The AL PURDY A-FRAME *Anthology*

The AL PURDY A-FRAME *Anthology*

Edited by Paul Vermeersch

with an introduction by Dennis Lee

HARBOUR PUBLISHING

In memory of Al Purdy
1918–2000

and for Eurithe Purdy

Harbour Publishing Co. Ltd.
P.O. Box 219, Madeira Park, BC, V0N 2H0
www.harbourpublishing.com

Cover photograph of Al Purdy by Kevin Kelly,
    www.kevinkellyphotography.com
Cover photograph of A-frame by Duncan Patterson
Edited by Paul Vermeersch and Silas White
Cover and text design by Anna Comfort
Map on page 8 by Teresa Karbashewski

Printed and bound in Canada

THE CANADA COUNCIL | LE CONSEIL DES ARTS
FOR THE ARTS | DU CANADA
SINCE 1957 | DEPUIS 1957

BRITISH
COLUMBIA
ARTS COUNCIL
We acknowledge the support of the Province of British Columbia
through the British Columbia Arts Council

Harbour Publishing acknowledges financial support from the
Government of Canada through the Book Publishing Industry
Development Program and the Canada Council for the Arts, and
from the Province of British Columbia through the BC Arts Council
and the Book Publishing Tax Credit.

Library and Archives Canada Cataloguing in Publication

The Al Purdy A-frame anthology / edited by Paul Vermeersch.

Includes bibliographical references.
ISBN 978-1-55017-502-8

1. Purdy, Al, 1918-2000. 2. Purdy, Al, 1918-2000—Appreciation.
3. Purdy, Al, 1918-2000—Literary collections. 4. Purdy, Al,
1918-2000—Homes and haunts—Ontario—Ameliasburgh. 5.
Canadian poetry (English)—20th century. 6. Canadian literature
(English)—21st century. 7. Poets, Canadian (English)—20th
century—Biography. I. Vermeersch, Paul

PS8531.U8Z557 2009   C810.8'0351
C2009-904037-9

So we built a house, my wife and I
our house at a backwater puddle of a lake
near Ameliasburg, Ont. spending
our last hard-earned buck to buy second-hand lumber
to build a second-hand house
and make a down payment on a lot
so far from anywhere
even homing pigeons lost their way
getting back from nowhere
we built a house so flagrantly noticeable
it seemed an act of despair
like the condemned man's bravado on the gallows
an A-frame house birds mistook for low blue sky
Just outside the cloud of my own black despair
was the small village a mile distant
once named Roblin's Mills

– Al Purdy
from "In Search of Owen Roblin"

Contents

Purdy Country

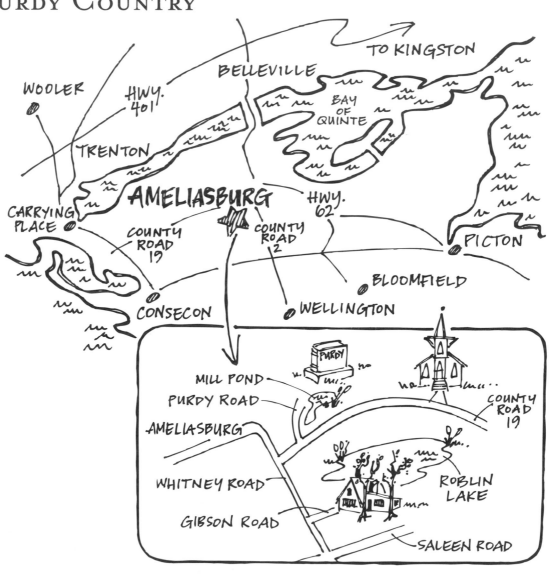

Publisher's Foreword

If this doesn't look quite like any book you've ever seen before—don't worry. You're not imagining it. It's a unique book on a unique subject. First of all, it's a book about a house. Not a very prepossessing house either—a backwoods cottage built from used lumber by a hard up couple who were approaching middle age at the end of a long string of disappointments. For over twenty years the man had tried to make it as a writer and the woman had tried to help him, but their long effort only appeared to confirm his mediocrity. But when they moved into their rough-hewn cottage, a truly remarkable thing happened. Nurtured by the deep connection he felt with this place the two of them forged with their own hands, the man began producing poems of startling originality. His newfound voice struck a note that reverberated across Canada and pilgrims began arriving at the backwoods cottage to acknowledge this unlikely master and perhaps carry a little of his creative spark away with them. The couple were glad of the company and met it with an enthusiasm that ensured more would come. For almost half a century it kept coming and the cottage became one of the most important crossroads on Canada's literary map. And the man kept writing brilliant, original poems, many of them celebrating the country around the cottage and the life it had opened to them, until he had produced what many consider the greatest body of poetry in Canadian literature.

This is the story of Al and Eurithe Purdy and their A-frame cottage in Ameliasburgh, Ontario. It is one of the great stories in Canadian letters and some of the country's most outstanding writers—prominently including the late, great Al Purdy himself—have combined their talents to tell it in these pages. They and the publisher have contributed their work free of charge so that all profit from the sale of this book can go into a fund to save the Purdy A-frame, which now sits empty, its future in doubt. One million dollars is needed to purchase the property, restore the buildings and administer it as a heritage property, possibly under Ontario Heritage. That comes to roughly 3 cents per Canadian, but fundraising is difficult in these recessionary times and success is by no means assured. We hope this book will help, both by raising cash and by making the case that the most significant writer's residence in the country deserves saving.

Howard White, CM, OBC
Harbour Publishing, Madeira Park, BC
October 2009

TILL THE HOUSE WAS REAL

Dennis Lee

This is a book about a house made from salvaged materials. About a nondescript piece of land, 100 feet by 265.

And about a tangle of literary friendships that flourished here, not to mention an incomparable poetic universe that grew from the house, the patch of ground, the neighbouring village, to take in all of Canada—opening further to vistas of planetary life, and millennial space and time. The whole shebang being as ad hoc and irreplaceable as the building where it began.

Which is to say, it's a book about the Purdy A-frame.

In July of 1957, Al and Eurithe Purdy bought an empty lot on tiny Roblin Lake. It looked across to Ameliasburg—one of the villages that dot Prince Edward County, the peninsula near the eastern end of Lake Ontario.

The Purdys were coming off a couple of years in Montreal, which had been something less than a triumph. Al was almost forty, a Grade 10 dropout with a quixotic compulsion to write verse. Now he'd met Irving Layton, Louis Dudek, Frank Scott, Milton Acorn; he was finally rubbing elbows with real poets. But his own work was hardly flourishing. He'd self-published a lamentable first collection thirteen years earlier, and had a total of two chapbooks

to show for his efforts since. And his new master plan—to support his family by writing radio plays for the CBC—wasn't going much better. They were barely getting by on Eurithe's earnings as a secretary. So when Al's mother became ill back in Trenton, Ontario, they moved in with her and started looking for a permanent place to live.

The lot they chose that July cost $800, two-thirds of their savings. And their decision to build the house themselves seemed foolhardy. Purdy could sort of hammer and saw; Eurithe had no construction experience at all. But they couldn't afford a professional builder. So they leafed

through a decorating magazine, liked the look of a small, cathedral-roof bungalow, wrote off for the manual, and set to work. And with strategic help from Jim Parkhurst (Eurithe's father) and Gordon (one of her brothers), they manhandled a basic structure into existence that summer and fall.

Lumber and concrete blocks came from a demolished government building in Belleville (there went another $500). Food was so scarce they scrounged for unopened cans in a nearby military dump; once they dined on rabbit à la roadkill. They commuted daily from Trenton, their son Jimmy going to school in Ameliasburg. And by that winter they had a house—albeit one with no insulation, electricity, or plumbing. To get water, Al had to chop through three feet of ice on the lake. Or maybe through four feet of ice… Whatever: that's how the story goes, and it might even be true—temperatures that winter were brutal. (Though on the other hand, Eurithe is no longer certain they spent the first winter there at all.)

The A-frame would be their home base for the next thirty years, till they moved to BC in 1987. And for a further ten years, they spent summers back at Roblin Lake. In the course of those four decades, the house would morph into legend—for its hospitality to other writers, complete with late-night brawls and epiphanies; for Purdy's mythologizing of the place in poem after poem; and for the quantum leap that occurred in his

writing there. Today the house is an improbable icon, a landmark in the country's imagining of itself, which calls out to be preserved.

But I'm jumping ahead. When spring came in 1958, the house was still half-built. They had no money. And Purdy was a bundle of nerves, frustrated by his poverty and the apparent dead end of his writing dreams. They kept working on the house, but in 1959 they had to retreat to Montreal for another year—Al to work in a mattress factory, Eurithe as a secretary at Parke-Davis. Soon they were back at Roblin Lake, however, and over the next decade they made a comfortable home,

When the house was finally ready to be lived in, conversations with friends on the sundeck became a regular event. Eurithe and Al recline at left.

with electricity and even indoor plumbing. (Though Al went on using the outhouse.)

They had help at times. In fact, one bit of lore has Purdy and Milton Acorn building the whole house together. This agreeable fantasy derives from "House Guest," a later poem that celebrates the cantankerous work sessions the two put in. But the sessions were few: two months in early 1960, and a woebegone week or so in 1962, after Milton and Gwendolyn MacEwen broke up. Eurithe's memory of the latter is that Milt hammered a few nails, and consumed a great deal of beer.

As the house was taking shape in those early years, a more obscure process was going on simultaneously. In a burst of high-speed growth, Purdy was turning into what many people—myself included—consider the finest poet English Canada has produced, and one of the enduring poets of the twentieth century.

How did it happen? The explanation remains inscrutable, but the evidence is clear. For a start, consider the opening lines of "Rattlesnake" (an early poem that kicks off his 1986 *Collected*). It shows the kind of thing he had to grow out of:

> An ominous length uncoiling and thin.
> A sliver of Satan annoyed by the din
> Of six berry-pickers, bare-legged and intent
> On stripping red treasure like rubies from Ghent.
> He moved without motion, he hissed without

> noise—
> A sombre dark ribbon that laughter destroys …

By 1957, Purdy had left these risible mannerisms behind. But he'd barely begun to inch into the gusto and freewheeling craft that would become his signature. Over the next six years at Roblin Lake, however, he would scribble like mad—and discover a music that carried from knockabout vernacular to a soaring high style. Listen to this, from "The Country North of Belleville":

> Old fences drift vaguely among the trees
>   a pile of moss-covered stones
> gathered for some ghost purpose
> has lost meaning under the meaningless sky
>   —they are like cities under water
> and the undulating green waves of time
>   are laid on them—

Somehow, in the midst of poverty, isolation and despair, Al Purdy had become a masterful poet. All the while imagining he could build a house, till the house was real. *Poems for All the Annettes*, his breakthrough collection, appeared in 1962; he finished the manuscript of *The Cariboo Horses* a year later. When the latter was published in 1965, it was greeted with a Governor General's Award, and the acclaim of other poets.

Dennis Lee

This extraordinary metamorphosis took place between 1957 and 1963—from Purdy at thirty-nine to Purdy at forty-five. In terms of poetry itself, it's the most compelling episode in the history of the house.

The A-frame Anthology, as you'll discover, is made up mostly of overlapping stories. My own favourite memory is of my first visit to Roblin Lake, probably in early 1968. I was the (extremely) novice editor at the House of Anansi, then barely a year old. And I'd written Purdy to ask if we could reissue *Annettes*, which had gone out of print at Contact Press. He not only agreed, he invited me down to Ameliasburg to discuss the details.

So I set out from Toronto one morning, buoyant but anxious. I'd met Purdy a few times, expecting to encounter the same broad range in the man   from corny to pensive to soulful—that I loved in the poetry. But no way. He was

Eurithe and Al in a home of their own at last, 1960s.

backslapping, argumentative, given to bumptious hijinks—and that was apparently it. The whole inward dimension of the poems didn't seem to be there; I couldn't even sense him protecting it, holding it in reserve. Which was a young man's naïveté, of course. But it left me leery. I was bringing along some editorial notes on *Annettes*; how would this slam-bang, six-pack Purdy react?

I arrived at noon, and we had some sandwiches Eurithe made. Then we toured the estate, with the requisite horseplay on both sides. But when we sat down with the poems, Al's manner changed. He'd been dubious about anyone editing his work, but there were clearly weaker pieces in the book. So we jockeyed ahead, with him dismissing some suggestions, pausing over others.

The best revisions happened when he set one of my bright ideas aside, but then came back—right away or later—with a far better move. Making the poems work was more important than anybody's ego, his or mine.

What struck me most during that session was his laser-beam focus. Along with a relaxed confidence in his craft. Gradually it dawned on me: this ferocious calm *was* the Purdy-of-many-dimensions I hadn't been able to locate. This was where the dazzling array of voices entered him. And if the sometimes awkward civilian was not in touch with the supple, wide-ranging poet who shared the same skin—so what?

I also remember a funny little two-step we got into. He had four new poems, written too late to be included in *Wild Grape Wine* (which McClelland & Stewart, by now his regular publisher, was bringing out that year). But he wanted to see the poems in a book, and he proposed that we smuggle them into the reprint of *Annettes*. He handed me some typed pages, and hitched his lanky frame back in the chair. One was "House Guest"; another was "At the Quinte Hotel." They flat out floored me. But there was a problem, he explained—a serious problem. Jack McClelland would undoubtedly collate the Contact and Anansi editions of *Annettes*, discover that four of the poems were new, and charge Purdy with violating his M&S contract. To head off this legal disaster, he had prepared a cover story. We would say that "House Guest" and the others were written years ago, but had been accidentally omitted in 1962. We were just restoring the book to its original form… I promised to vouch for every word of this baloney, and in the poems went.

Though surprisingly, when *Annettes* came out McClelland never raised the matter at all.

The rest of the visit is a blur. But I remember driving home that night; the car scarcely needed gas. A wonderful poet was entrusting this landmark book to Anansi, and he'd let me a hair's-breadth into his working space. As I flew along the darkened 401, my whole body was singing. As it did all the way to T.O.

Like the house itself, *The A-frame Anthology* is an improvised structure. Apart from Purdy's poems and reminiscences, most of the pieces were written for this volume. And they're a patchwork quilt—by turns anecdotal, analytic, affectionate. At some points they overlap, but they don't always agree on details. And of course there are gaps, since the story can never be complete. The whole thing makes for an exhilarating read.

Mind you, there are two inconsistencies which may puzzle a reader. If you find Purdy's chronology vague at times, even contradictory, you're right. He recognized the problem himself; it will be up to a biographer to nail down dates with precision.

A larger question is this: did the Purdys live in Ameliasburg, or Ameliasburgh? As far as I can tell, it's like this. They lived in Ameliasburgh-with-an-"h" Township (though it ceased to exist in 1998, when Prince Edward County became a single-tier municipality). As for the village, the "h" and "non-h" spellings are used interchangeably by locals—a free-form tradition which Purdy follows with scrupulous care.

There's a common conviction behind the yarns and tributes here: *we must preserve the A-frame.* This is the most storied writer's house in Canada. And because so many of the poems written here explore the length and breadth of the country, the house itself has become a living password, a concrete reminder of who and what we are. It would be folly to lose a totem of such power; we can't afford such cultural amnesia.

Fortunately, there's a campaign to save the A-frame. It's spearheaded by Jean Baird, with Eurithe's blessing. The goal is to purchase the Purdy house and endow it as a permanent writers' retreat. This volume, with all its profits going to the fund, is one step in that campaign.

But there's more to be done, and it's urgent. Please be sure to read the final piece in *The A-frame Anthology*. You'll find more details about the campaign, and suggestions for how you can contribute. I hope you will; you'll put generations to come in your debt.

As we are all in debt—to Al Purdy.

Dennis Lee
June 2009, Toronto

AN OPEN LETTER

Stan Dragland

September 11, 2008

To Whom It May Concern,

Al Purdy's house in Ameliasburgh is a house full of stories. It's the only house to which I've ever made a pilgrimage, and that was when Al was alive. I'm no literary pilgrim, but I did visit Al with Michael Ondaatje once and a couple of times on my own, at Al's invitation. Our first contact was in 1976, when he wrote to ask if he could get a copy of *Wilson MacDonald's Western Tour* from me. We made an exchange. I got *Sundance at Dusk* ("for Stan Dragland, dragger out of things from under stones & [illegible] & time, with most cordial greetings from Al Purdy, Nov 20, 76. Ameliasburg"). Al was one hell of a book collector. It was really something to see his library of Canadian books, and to sit with him in the study where he wrote his poems and essays and letters. I'm no worshipper of great ones, as I say, and no habitual visitor of them. I'm almost always content just to read them. But I made an exception for Al, so I was there one afternoon, the day before he was to leave on a reading tour.

It was late fall, or late winter. I don't remember which, but there was snow on the ground. Al asked me to help haul a huge log into his fireplace to keep the place warm while he was away. Log isn't quite right. This was a large piece of tree. It was about three feet of trunk, easily a foot and a half in diameter. It wouldn't fit lengthwise, so we shoved it end-wise into the fire so that most of it hung out on the floor. I had my doubts about the strategy. Why wouldn't the log burn out into the living room and catch the whole place on fire? Goodbye A-frame. Goodbye potential shrine. But that was Al's business. Mine was to shut up and help with the lifting.

Al's house is still there. It should have burned down, but it didn't. Maybe Al shouldn't have been a good poet either, self-taught as he was. He improvised his poems like he improvised his heating. But he got to be one of the best poets of his generation, and he was so gregarious that he became a vortex of cultural energy that was an

irresistible attraction to literary types like me. Al and I did some drinking together while he was writer-in-residence at the University of Western Ontario, where I taught. Later I wrote an essay on his poetry. Later still, I had the honour of serving as his editor for *Naked With Summer in Your Mouth*. And after his death I made another pilgrimage, this one to his resting place in Ameliasburgh cemetery, with Phil Hall, another of his grateful inheritors. As soon as I can, I'm going to visit his statue at Queen's Park in Toronto.

The omphalos of Purdy's world was Ameliasburgh and Roblin Lake. He made the place sing to his readers, and his poems sing to new readers still, which is why it's appropriate that his statue stands in the centre of Toronto,

another centre of the country he loved so much. But at the navel of the world he both lived in and created stands the house he built with his own hands at a time in his life when it looked like he was getting nowhere in the writing world. It's packed with stories. A dear shaggy spirit haunts it. For the love of that huge, indelible presence, and for the good of our collective soul, let's make damn sure it's preserved.

Stan Dragland

The A-frame was always well stocked with books. These bookshelves are in the A-frame's bedroom. More were around the walls of the living room and in the detached library.

To Build a House!

Al Purdy

Roblin Lake was turquoise and dazzling blue in mid-summer. Orioles, robins, sparrows, swallows and goldfinches thronged our living space, which was also *their* living space. One morning on first arrival I saw a great blue heron stalking the shore, an ungainly native. And we saw muskrats. They pushed a wave ahead of them with their noses while swimming. It was idyllic. I looked at the delightful Eden landscape and longed for the grimy streets of Montreal. I was not a country guy, but a sallow-complexioned cigar-puffing expatriate banished from the big city. It must have showed in my permanently dismayed expression at Ameliasburgh—I hate beautiful trees. Eurithe interrupted my contemplation of them: "Get to work!" The tone was imperative.

To build a house! My own carpentering skills were nearly minimal (I could saw a board more or less straight, and pound a nail without always bending it); Eurithe's were non-existent. We'd come across some architect's plans in *House Beautiful* magazine that appealed to both of us, a small A-frame structure with adjoining kitchen and bath. It didn't look like every other house around Roblin Lake. But in order to build on our lot, we had to prepare the land: it was a jungle of willows. So I became a temporary lumberjack, chopping, sawing and burning.

When negotiations had been underway to buy the land, the lot adjoining ours appealed to us; it had a shoreline that projected out into Roblin Lake. But Harry Gibson charged by the foot for the entire winding length of that shoreline, instead of the straight-across footage that would have cost much less. Therefore we opted for the nearby straight-across and more affordable lot. Later on we intended to build our own handmade peninsula, by wheelbarrow and muscle. (After ten years we had extended our small kingdom out into the lake about forty feet.)

After pondering, lubrication and cogitation, we enlarged the house-plan foundation to thirty feet long and seventeen feet wide. The A-frame section was eighteen feet high, measuring from the floor to gable. It was erected on four-foot walls. The finished house at that point was entirely in our heads, of course. And I've come more and more to realize: without Jim Parkhurst's help, it could never have been done.

His character was phlegmatic and almost unbearably calm; mine was excitable and ever mercurial. I'd come to him sometimes, despairing and despondent with an insoluble problem. The difficulty would melt away and seem never to have existed; do this and do that in the ordinary course of building. It was almost possible for me to think I'd solved the puzzle myself; but not quite. He'd drive to the lake from Belleville once or twice a week, listen to our woeful account of difficulties. Our troubles simply disappeared in the face of his unchanging calm.

As will be obvious, I pondered the man. His mind worked on a different level than mine; he wasn't self-aware in quite the same way. To say that he was concrete and I abstract wouldn't explain it: he could at least imagine what our house should be, shadowy in his own pragmatic mind, ordinary as a bent nail. Whereas I thought the projected house was something marvellous, a factual dream of solidity. I think, therefore I am: I think a house and ergo the house am?

There was always a reserve about him, a foreignness even; some kind of dirt-poor grassroots aristocracy, a northern nobility I couldn't quite conceive. And of course I'm embroidering a bit here, searching for something about the man that may not exist at all. But I must forgive myself for doing it, since I'm saying as much about myself as about him.

Early summer, 1957, Eurithe and I stand near the shores of Roblin Lake. We measure the supposedly equal sides of our house-footing with diagonal lines. That is, we stretch a cord kitty-corner from and to opposite ends of wooden forms. Then we switch sides and do the opposite. This in order that all angles, lengths and widths should match and measure true. All this time, orioles and robins plunge the sun-bright air around us. They build their nest houses in playful joy and love without measuring a damn thing; ourselves in worry and suspense and labour. I grin at the thought, promptly messing up our diagonal measurements, forgetting to keep the lines taut.

The Purdys pose in front of their semi-finished house.

Sometimes all the studding, fireboard, planks and nails dance in my head, like those ephemeral little flies that dance in bright sunlight. A dance of nothingness it seemed to me. And I felt dubious about the house ever being built. And I must do things I do for their own sake, their own worthwhileness. Anything else was illusory. The poems I wrote must live in themselves, exist as entities and dance in their own sunlight. Without an audience, minus acclaim, even from a few. Thinking such things is treading gingerly close to a fifty-thousand-gallon tank of bullshit, teetering even. I wallow and rejoice in self-pity, my stiff upper lip is a dirty dishrag. In short, we built a house.

Among the most awful clichés that litter your mind: "it was the best of times, it was the worst of times"—But yeah, it was. Both. The house became a ragged cobweb against the sky. We moved in long before it was finished; still isn't. Eurithe and I poured concrete for the footings with a

non-musical throb of cement mixer pounding our nerves. And we quarrelled. About damn near everything. Name something we didn't quarrel over, and I still can't be sure we didn't.

But the house was important. We never thought of it that way, but it was. Our lives were involved and wrapped up in that silly old house. Survival. When food gets scarce, that word survival lurks in the near periphery. Sure, Eurithe could have left me and taken safe refuge with her family in Belleville. But what kind of disgraceful defeat is that? You live, this is the way it is; make a fuss if you don't like; scream at the world a little, exaggerate everything like I'm doing now. (Am I really?)

In the family room, looking up to the interior peak of the A-frame.

Interruption

Al Purdy

When the new house was built
callers came:
black squirrels on the roof every morning
between sleep and wakefulness,
and a voice saying "Hello dead man."
A chipmunk looks in the window
and I look out,
the small face and the large one
waver together in glass,
but neither moves
while the leaves turn into shadows.
Orioles, robins and red-winged blackbirds
are crayons that colour the air;
something sad and old
cries down in the swamp.
Moonlight in the living room,
a row of mice single file
route marching across the empty lunar plain
until they touch one of my thoughts
and jump back frightened,
but I don't wake up.

Pike in the lake pass and re-pass the windows
with clouds in their mouth.
For 20 minutes every night
the sun slaps a red paint brush
over dinner dishes and leftovers,
but we keep washing it off.
Birds can't take a shortcut home
they have to fly around the new house;
and cedars grow pale green candles
to light their way thru the dark.
Already the house is old:
a drowned chipmunk (the same one?)
in the rain barrel this morning,
dead robins in the roof overhang,
and the mice are terrified—
We have set traps,
and must always remember
to avoid them ourselves.

At Roblin Lake

Linda Rogers

I have dealt with brothers and sons, boys who dipped my pigtails in inkwells and put itching powder down my neck at school, and the bullies down the lane who ran away when I chased them "bear style," banging a piece of kindling on our garbage can lid.

I knew how to handle Al. Eurithe knew how to handle Al. We waited like cats and pounced at the right moment. He could be brought down with the right words, and, born into a family of lawyers, I had been a debater in high school and university.

At Roblin Lake, we argued over food and who was and was not a good poet or a good singer. As far as Al was concerned, almost all the good cooks, poets and singers (they *are* related) were men.

I have enjoyed many great meals cooked by Eurithe, who is a traditional cook, just as her husband was a traditional man; but Al always found fault with something she had made, at least until the end of his life. Then, I noticed, he was gentler. "She controls my oxygen," he said, gloomily pointing to the cylinder that held his breath.

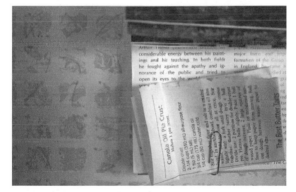

One of the great joys of Roblin Lake was chasing the wild asparagus. Al knew every secret location, no matter whose property it was on. He had the rights of seniority. It was his rural hood and he had the prerogatives of a local boy. Still, we treated the experience like a bank robbery. Eurithe drove the getaway car (How come so many male poets make their wives do the driving?). She'd stop on a loonie while her great hunter-gatherer would unfold his endless limbs, fling open the door and race to the tender shoots, one step ahead

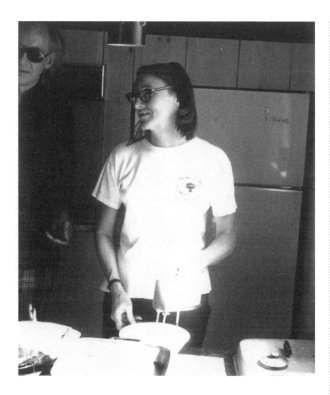

Eurithe prepares a meal, perhaps with wild asparagus, as Al looks on. The kitchen was cramped but had a formidable reputation for producing abundant fare on short notice.

The best time at the lake is the early morning. I got up and started the sponge with Eurithe. We'd make her ornery husband cinnamon buns for breakfast. The bread was rising in one of her plastic mixing bowls. It was time for me to take my morning swim in the lake. "Don't worry," I said. "This is a slow method but it never fails."

It was beautiful in the water, and I swam for miles.

When I got back to the A-frame, hungry and ready for the last punch and rise, the addition of raisins and brown sugar, Eurithe was doubled over the kitchen counter, either laughing or crying. It was hard to tell because her house was full of smoke and those little black bits that float around when plastic is burned.

"I thought I'd hurry up the bread by putting it in the oven to rise," she said between gasps, pointing to the sculptural object that was half melted bowl and half dough.

We tiptoed into the master bedroom. Her baby-faced husband was snoring like the Mormon Tabernacle Choir. "Open the windows and doors," I whispered. "Spray the place with Canadian Club."

We had bacon and eggs for breakfast, and Al never found out.

of farmers with rifles. We'd take off, leaving rubber, with the door hanging open.

The asparagus was delicious and the poems were good. I think the process is somewhat similar.

Poor Eurithe. Our defensive strategy was undone by bread. As a thank you for hospitality, if my host or hostess is interested, I share my secret for successful bread, using the surefire sponge method. I may have gathered some bad reviews in my time, but no one has ever criticized my bread, not even Al.

A Permanent Emergency

Al Purdy

The house was still a skeleton without flesh in the autumn of 1957: flesh being insulation, siding, paint and other amenities. An old cookstove in the A-frame living room supplied heat. We had scrounged coal oil lamps for light (there was no electricity). Three of those lamps, clustered together, if you read a book, meant your eyes wouldn't fall out of your head. But they were a smoky dangerous fire hazard right out of the nineteenth century. When winter came like a lion, tiger and tyrannosaurus combined, the lake we used for water became armored with ice—ice three-foot-plus thick in March.

I chopped through it with an axe all that first winter. In March, you had to chop a four- or five-foot circle in the ice, narrowing at the bottom to produce a huge funnel, from which water leaped upward in a reverse cataract at the final downward blow. I'd be sweating profusely as the work proceeded in fairly mild winter weather, discarding pieces of clothing one by one. At the end I'd often be stripped down to shorts. Mrs. Eley, observing me from her kitchen window, said I was "Mr. Tarzan." This flattered me inordinately.

The surface of our lives was tolerable, bearable, even enjoyable and producing occasional laughter at times. We were healthy, all three of us were, and a damn good thing too. Our original Montreal grubstake of some twelve hundred bucks had melted away, leaving a few measly dollars hoarded against emergencies. But ours was a permanent emergency.

A small chapbook of my poems was published that year by Fred Cogswell at the University of New Brunswick. He probably felt sorry for me; and now I think that little book was simply bad. (Alden Nowlan produced a much superior first book of his own the following year.) And I did a lot of writing in 1957. But poems about this traumatic period for me didn't appear until much later, during the early 1960s.

Winter, 1957. The county forests turned a brilliant scarlet and gold; the sky of autumn filled with hundreds of thousands of migrating Canada geese, squawking ceaselessly. And winter appeared without transition, Indian summer directly to frozen lake and miles of snow. We had to wake up at three-hour intervals through the night to stoke the cookstove, when the temperature plunged far below zero. A few feet from the stove, wind whistled through openings I had neglected to caulk. My deficiencies as a house-builder were very obvious.

Outside was white-magic: trees clothed in wedding gowns of snow, or a rattling armour of ice after freezing rain. When the lake had been in the process of freezing, partly covered with sheets of ice, wind lifted the ice at intervals, producing a sound like extra-terrestrial animals wanting to return home. In deep winter and sinking temperatures, ice cracked with a terrifying noise, as if a god were scourging the earth.

In the morning, when you emerged bleary-eyed from the many-times interrupted sleep to piss, the white damask was scrolled with a delicate tracery of art work—animal footprints, birds' hieroglyphics, your own deep yellow calligraphy. Empty by day, the cold world was populated by rabbits, stray cats and dogs, squirrels and chipmunks by night.

But even in winter, the weather sometimes turned suddenly warm. I remember one occasion like a spring evening, except that flakes of snow were drifting down softly as dandelion parachutes, and there was a luminous quality about the lighting. As if the white blanket was internally glowing, and a convention of white fireflies had decided that here was the place they wanted to sleep.

I was getting ready for bed, had removed all my clothes. Then, on a whim, I put on my shoes and went outside into the falling world. It was like being caressed by little white sparks, the touch no more than a ghostly awareness of touching. The feeling of having once had wings, or an additional sense beyond the ordinary five which enabled the possessor to be part of things instead of separate from them. But after five minutes or so the cold attacked my naked body, a thickening of perception and slowing down of movement. Retreating into the house, I felt as if I had glimpsed a human faculty we had lost when life was "nasty, brutish and short," but you could speak to snowflakes in their own language…

Money was an absent guest, a necessity we didn't have. We were short of food, the car was empty of gasoline. Eurithe and I talked it over. "I'll have to hitchhike to Montreal and get a job," I said. "Maybe," she said, "but not now, not when it's so cold."

So I delayed my departure until it got warmer. But it didn't get warmer. After a bleak Christmas in which there were no gifts but good wishes that didn't cost money, January was a continual Ice Age. I refused to think of how cold it was.

Eurithe said don't go. I went, bundled up in scarf and overcoat; but no gloves; I had none.

It was Sunday. There were friends in Montreal with whom I expected to find refuge. The sun shone like steel; cold cut like a knife. I got a ride to Belleville. Another Shannonville on #2 Highway. Then a long wait, and another twenty-mile hop eastward. One kindly motorist, noticing I had nothing on my hands in this bitter weather, gave me a pair of gloves. I was almost weepily sentimental thanking him. And I reached Kingston by noon of that January Sunday, while people went to church and prayed to the God of their fathers… I stood by the roadside with thumb extended, wondering if it would help to pray a little. And decided it wouldn't.

Another ride to Gananoque, twenty miles east of Kingston. And there I stalled. Standing on the side of the road for an hour, for an hour and a half, for two hours, I lost track of time. Cold bored into my body; I jumped up and down to relieve numbness in feet and legs; I tried to think good thoughts and thoughts of food. I had eaten the sandwich lunch in my pocket, but food-thoughts made me hungry again.

After how long a time at Gananoque I don't know, and after no motorist even slowing down to examine me curiously, I switched sides of the road and attempted to hitchhike back the way I had come. At that point I was feeling desperate and despairing, very, very sorry for myself.

The switch worked. I got a ride right away, and another after that. I walked the last six miles home. And entered the house ashamed. I suppose that amusing anecdote was my low point.

I'm bound to over-dramatize it, of course. But it's difficult to do that with the nadir, and what's lower than the low?—foolish grandiloquent writer reduced to penury, crying in his beer if he had beer. "Corpse discovered near Gananoque on the #2 Highway?" "Whaddaya think, Eurithe?" "Would you like some hot soup, dear?"

Spring came, the birds returned, dandelions bloomed, frogs sang on the shores of Roblin Lake. The mating season, flashes of colour in the air, green and yellow on the ground, the sky blue and grey with sun and rain. Our financial situation was no better, but we survived.

Winter at Roblin Lake

Al Purdy

Seeing the sky darken & the fields
turn brown & the lake lead-grey
as some enormous scrap of sheet metal
& wind grabs the world around the equator
I am most thankful then for knowing about
    the little gold hairs on your belly

From "As the Dream Holds the Real"

Russell Morton Brown

In the 1970s, not long after my first encounter with Canadian poetry, I went to a reading by Al Purdy. And didn't like it. Purdy's delivery was a loud grumble that seemed addressed more to himself than to his audience. And his voice trailed off so much as he reached his closing lines that it was as if all the poems ended with anticlimaxes. I was therefore not surprised, when his letters were later published, to learn that Purdy didn't like reading in public. However, by then I had heard him read many times and had become quite fond of the experience. For that to happen, I had to learn how to hear his poetry and to understand that there was something about his language—both spoken and written that was uniquely his. The rhythms in his poems were different (looser, less formal) from those I'd previously tuned my ear to. And the last lines of his poems often *were* anticlimaxes. I had to learn, in short, what was at stake in a Purdy poem—and why ending on a falling note had its own kind of power.

About a decade after first hearing him read, I had the good fortune to become the editor of his first *Collected Poems*. So in the spring and summer of 1985, I made weekly trips to the house he had built for himself and his wife Eurithe on the edge of Roblin Lake—a well made little cottage with a detached one-room study for solitude when Purdy wanted to read or write. We didn't work on the book there, but at his kitchen table. To my surprise, our discussions often consisted of my arguing for poems that Purdy was ready to discard—poems that seemed to me necessary to preserve in a volume representing what ought to be saved from an extraordinary career.

Purdy was also not satisfied with some of the poems he thought *should* be included. A compulsive reviser, he tinkered with old lines still. Several times we went back over previously published versions of a poem to see which one he now preferred. (One of these poems had changed so radically in the revision that I persuaded him to include both the original and altered state.) He

The A-frame living room, adjacent to kitchen and hall.

told me the perhaps apocryphal story of how, after spending a day revising two poems at once, he had moved so many lines from one to the other and vice versa that he finally exchanged their titles as well. Our project moved forward slowly because Purdy loved to tell such stories and to reminisce about his encounters with other writers. He would also stop to recite poems that our work had brought to mind. In the vast storehouse he had committed to memory it was not surprising to find D.H. Lawrence along with other modernists; however, I discovered that he also had great quantities of Tennyson that he loved to recall.

Eurithe put in occasional appearances to tell her husband that he was being foolish about something or to put out a plate with the Scottish oatcakes he liked to snack on while we worked. We sipped coffee or water because Purdy had given up drinking by then. He also no longer smoked.

Our first editing session was approached in a circuitous fashion. After Purdy picked me up at the Belleville train station, he told me we couldn't go back to his house yet because he had noticed asparagus ferns on the way over. Hours later, after touring the countryside and grubbing through roadside ditches, we finally

pulled into his driveway around twilight. I like to think that before we could enter the cooked world of poetry and publishing, he had wanted to affirm the raw world of physical appetite. And perhaps remind me that in Purdy-country some food didn't come from supermarket bins.

Purdy's poems document a life divided between the poles of intellect and the physical world: they show a world of experience enlivened by unseen and invisible presences—often brought there by the poet's own acute awareness of the past. In poems such as "Inside the Mill" he tells us how the speaker wants us to notice the spectres of presences that are "transparent as shadows" as well as the ruined physical building that remains. "When you cross the doorway you feel them/ when you cross the places they've been/ there's a flutter of time in your heartbeat/ of time going backward and forward." This is poetry that teaches us how "one illusion balanced another/ as the dream holds the real in proportion."

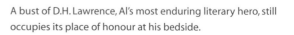

A bust of D.H. Lawrence, Al's most enduring literary hero, still occupies its place of honour at his bedside.

Prince Edward County

Al Purdy

Words do have smell and taste
these have the taste of apples
brown earth and red tomatoes
as if a juggler had juggled
too many balls of fire
and dropped some of them
a smell and taste and bell sound
in the ear of waves
—not princes

Conservative since the Romans
—altho it's only animals
that are true conservatives
using the same land and water
and air for countless generations
themselves their own ancestors
each their own child
rabbits and groundhog tenants
porcupine leaseholders
and the wide estates of foxes

This is an island and you know
it's like being dressed in lace
as only a woman may be
and not be laughed at
around her neck and throat
the silver dance of coastlines
and bells rung deep in limestone

Animals having no human speech
have not provided names
but named it with their bodies
and the long-ago pine forests
named it with their bodies
and the masts of sailing ships
around the century's turn
named it to the sea
and a bird one springtime
named it bobolink bobolink
even a small unremarkable flower
I saw last April blossoming
that died shortly after
named it for herself
trillium

And we—the latecomers
white skins and brown men
no voice told us to stay
but we did for a lifetime
of now and then forever
the fox and flower and rabbit
and bells rung deep in limestone
—for any who come after
you have heard our names
and the word we made of silence
bobolink and—

This Inn Is Free

F.R. Scott

I will arise and go now, and go to Roblin Lake,
To a cottage NORTH OF SUMMER, with PURDY on the door.
I'll arm myself with hard-tack, some rat-poison, and steak,
And sleep alone on a hard-wood floor.

When dawn comes through the window, with bird-song *à la crow*,
I'll rise and light my candle, and search for things I love,
And wrapping round my blanket, to warm me as I go
I'll creep my way to the unlit stove.

When AL comes down to join me, I'll greet him with a grin.
My books will all be ready, my voice will be so sure,
That though he'll try reciting before I can begin
I'll blast him with my OVERTURE.

Then will the lists be open, the poems laid on the line.
Before MY EYE OF THE NEEDLE, his skill shall not prevail,
Though he try to make me sodden with gallons of WILD GRAPE WINE,
And set his CARIBOO HORSES on my tail.

Oh I can't wait to visit the igloo of the soul
Where Acorns, Birneys, Newloves, and bards of equal fame
Have plastered both themselves and every leaking hole

And warmed their hearts at PURDY's flame.

ONTARIO

Al Purdy

Rural Ontario is a nice place to visit. It's also a nice place to live. My wife and I built a house on Roblin Lake near Ameliasburgh twenty years ago, and the "natives" still regard us as outsiders. People around there have voted Conservative since the last shot was fired in the American Revolution, which was when the United Empire Loyalists first started to arrive. And I have no doubt that those first arrivals looked snootily down their noses at the last johnny-come-latelies.

We built the house with a pile of used lumber bought in nearby Belleville, then went inside to wait out the winter. We had no electricity or plumbing. Three oil lamps were required to read a book, and I chopped through three- and four-foot-thick ice for water come February and March. An ancient iron cookstove was the only heat source. In really cold weather, I set the alarm clock for every two hours so that I could climb out of bed and stoke the stove. The neighbours, of course, thought I was plumb crazy and my wife even crazier to stay with me.

But while living there—trapped, if you like—I was forced to explore my own immediate surroundings. In 1957 the old Roblin grist-mill was still standing—an enormous ruined hulk four stories high, with three-foot thick stone walls. I poked into every corner of that mill, stepping gingerly over black holes in the floor that dropped forty feet straight down, marvelling at the twenty-four-inch-wide boards from vanished green forests. Old Owen Roblin built that grist-mill in 1842. Around 1960 they tore out its liver and lights, installing them in Black Creek Pioneer Village just outside Toronto for the edification of tourists.

Wandering the roads on foot or driving when we had money for gas, I got interested in old architecture—not as an expert, but with the idea that houses express the character of long-dead owners and builders. Gingerbread woodwork on a white frame house, for instance: the exact spot where nineteenth-century man worked an hour longer than he had to because he got interested and forgot about

money. That lost nineteenth-century hour
is still visible at one corner of the house.

I keep finding roads I never noticed before,
even after all these years of being an outsider—as
if some celestial roads department built them
last night in the dark of the moon. Leafy and
overgrown some of them, fading to a green dead
end at run-down farmhouses, abandoned long
since but still containing the map of people's
lives. Roads like tunnels under trees to thick
that the sun shatters into splinters among black
branches. Country roads have this endearing
quality of never going anywhere important,
certainly not to a city, of being an end in
themselves, as if at any place where you might
care to stop the car you have already arrived.

Typical Purdy Country scenery along Gibson Road near the A-frame

Next page: Al and Eurithe do the "Canadian Gothic."

IF THOSE WALLS COULD TALK

A Reminiscence by Eurithe Purdy
recorded and edited by Howard White

Interviewer's note: I collected the comments below by following Eurithe Purdy around southern Vancouver Island for three days in July 2009, as she prepared to sell the waterfront home in Sidney where she and Al had spent their winters through the 1990s. At eighty-five Eurithe was lean, focused, and hard to keep up with, even for someone twenty years younger. Rather than call in a dumpster as I once did in a similar situation, she was conducting an exhausting multi-day yard sale, laboriously disposing of a houseful of old shoes, clothes, books, typewriters, sofas and assorted flotsam. She kept all the tools, expecting to make good use of them at her new, smaller home in Victoria. She admitted the yard sale was hardly worth it for the money, but took satisfaction knowing some artifacts from her life with Al would continue to be used and appreciated. Most of our conversation was wedged into the early hours before the sale started and the evenings after the goods had been boxed, covered and moved out of the rain, followed by a late supper of freezer pizza. I asked her how she managed, not just to survive all those years on nothing but Al's earnings as a poet, but to acquire a couple of nice houses along the way.

"I am very frugal," she said.

Frugal not just with money, but also with words. On reading over this interview she was surprised at how much she had said, and not entirely comfortable with the effect I had created by removing my side of the conversation, which could give the false impression she rambles on a bit. I considered leaving some of my musings in, but unfortunately they did little to illumine the subject of the A-frame, which I visited only once, and that long after Al had left the building. I am afraid I must ask Eurithe to settle for my avowal that in real life she speaks with admirable economy, and made these comments over the course of three busy days while her mind was on many other things.

– Howard White

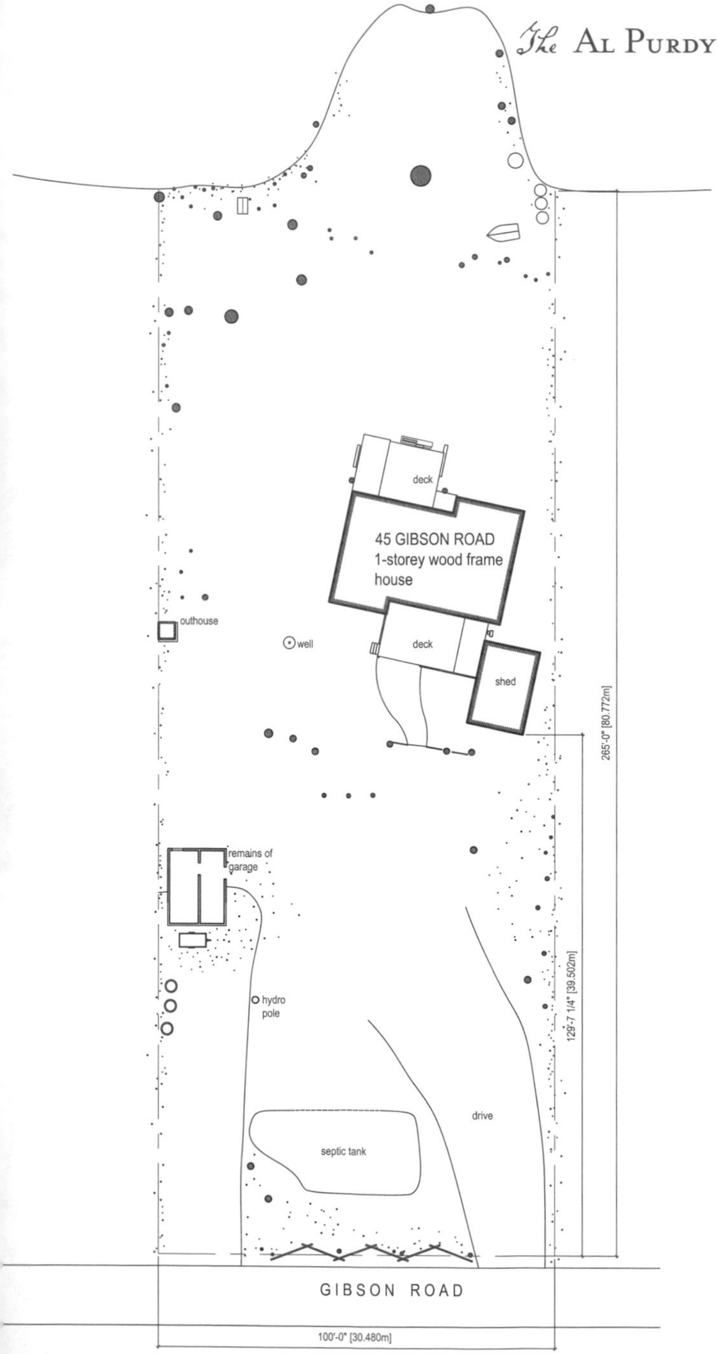

The site plan diagram contains the following labels:

- deck
- 45 GIBSON ROAD 1-storey wood frame house
- outhouse
- well
- deck
- shed
- remains of garage
- hydro pole
- septic tank
- drive
- GIBSON ROAD
- 265'-0" [80.772m]
- 129'-7 1/4" [39.502m]
- 100'-0" [30.480m]

I n 1957 Al and I decided to move back home. We had grown up in southeastern Ontario, he in Trenton and I in Belleville, and we had been moving around since we got married in 1941. During the war we had moved to Vancouver while Al was stationed there with the Air Force, then when the war ended and our son Jimmy was born we went back to Belleville where Al got involved in running a taxi business with my dad, Jim Parkhurst. In 1946 or '47 Al and I had the first of many splits—we actually got divorced and he married my girlfriend Ila Bachelor, and they had a son they named Brian. But after a year or so Al and I got together again and moved back to Vancouver. We stayed there until 1955, Al working at a slaughterhouse and a mattress factory and me doing secretarial work when I wasn't busy raising Jimmy. Then we moved to Montreal where Al got involved in the local poetry scene with Irving Layton, Frank Scott, Ron Everson, Louis Dudek, Milton Acorn and others and I worked for the CPR. But Al's mother back in Trenton was getting quite frail, and we were ready to try living back on home turf again so in 1957 we moved in with her in Al's childhood home. That was impossible, for Al more than me,

Left: Site Plan of the A-frame property. Drawing by Duncan Patterson.

Opposite: The family room.

40

so we started looking for a place of our own.

We didn't have much money so my dad suggested we get a piece of bare land and build our own house. We drove up and down backroads around Trenton until we spotted this lot that suited our budget across Roblin Lake from Ameliasburgh. I think it was $800 or thereabouts. Actually we wanted the lot next door to the one we bought, because it had a small point jutting out into the lake that looked like a good place to swim and build a dock, but the farmer who was selling it, a man named Gibson, insisted on charging by the foot of lake frontage, which made the one with the straight shoreline quite a bit cheaper. In time we built our own jetty out into the lake, while the natural point on the lot we had wanted got washed away, so it was just as well. We didn't realize it at the time but the land along that stretch of shoreline was subject to flooding. It had been under water at an earlier time, but the lake level had gone down and exposed it. We built it up with fill Al hauled in with my dad's truck but there were times that the water came up right around the house during runoff, though it never actually reached the floor.

Al and I decided to build an A-frame and found a plan that suited us in a magazine. A frames were quite novel at that time and I guess it appealed to us because it wasn't like every other cottage. Looking back, it was impractical. So much waste space. The corners where the walls met the floor were practically unusable, although we built cabinets there, low ones. And the high peak of the ceiling was just useless. You couldn't even reach it to clean it. We did fill part of it with a sleeping loft, but that was so cramped you only had room to stand up in the very middle. It could only be used by the young and agile because you had to climb up a ladder. I think Pat Lane might have used it, when he was a young fellow. We never did. Jimmy slept in the second bedroom when he was with us.

One of the things that attracted people to A-frames is that they appeared to be simple to build, but they're not really. You have those long rafters to stand up, which is tricky, everything has to be cut on angles, and the roof is too steep to work on easily. It would be okay in a place where there is heavy snow, but it doesn't make sense anywhere else. We salvaged materials from a building demolition in Belleville for a lot of it, but we ended up having to buy the rafters new because of the dimensions. And of course with an A-frame most of the exterior is made up of roof, and we had to buy duroid roofing to cover all of that.

We could never have built it without my family's assistance. They helped in so many ways. My brother Gordon was working at the CPR yard and was able to get his hands on a lot of odd-sized lumber that was being thrown away. A lot of it was BC fir, and was that ever hard. It bent the nails. A lot of bent nails and cracked fingers. A lot of swear words, too. We scrounged building materials everywhere. The siding came from an old barn that blew down one winter—it must date back to the late 1800s. There's some really old wood in that house.

My dad was the key to the building of that place. He had the knowledge and he did a lot of the work. Dad was an odd-job person. He did carpentry, he did electrical, he did plumbing, trucking, all that sort of thing—when he wasn't playing poker and losing money. He was a strong man. He and Al got along—sort of. I can't remember if my other brother Lawrence worked on the original A-frame or not. He may not have—he may have been in the debt-collection business at that time—but he became a master builder later and helped us with improvements. Oh gosh, he does wonderful work. He is meticulous. I have one nephew like that, too. It's amazing what they can do with wood. It didn't rub off on me, unfortunately. I can saw a board. I can nail a board. I can do quite a lot actually. But not fine stuff.

Al wasn't a natural when it came to carpentry either, or any kind of manual work really, but he did pitch in. When he worked at the mattress factory, that was hard work. When he worked at the slaughtering place in Vancouver, that was hard work. Whatever he did, he did it with his whole heart. When he did the building that he did and the carpentry that he did, he was right there 100 percent. There was always something in the head, though. Another poem being written. So the mind is there, always there. I marvelled at that. How do you get that way? My thoughts are usually on the practical plane. I'm never away up there in the stratosphere. Even back before his poetry became something that somebody else would want to read, he was just as much that way as later, when he was better known. I marvelled at it. And he did. Wonder at it. Where did it come from? There was nothing in his family background to account for it. Neither of us had any relatives who were involved in the arts. I'm sure there was some grumbling in my family about Al's big ideas of becoming a writer instead of settling down and making a respectable living and I got impatient sometimes but I never doubted that it was worth it in the long run. Even at a young age I knew that his kind of dedication wasn't in vain.

I have to laugh when I read that the A-frame was built by two poets—Al and Milton Acorn. It makes a good story, but the truth is Milton was only there for a few weeks, and not that much got done. I did far more carpentry on that house than Milton ever did. I probably did as much work as Al, overall. I kept at it after Al had sort of given up on it. The flat-roofed part, the big addition we put on in the mid-seventies, Al wasn't involved in that. I'm not sure why. Maybe it was done when he was on a trip that I didn't go on. He was in on the planning of course. I was probably more pushing for it than he, but he certainly didn't object. As long as he wasn't included in the building of it. I think one of my cousins helped us and Lawrence, who had become an expert builder by this time, had quite a lot to do with the building of that section. I don't think we bothered with plans for that part—just sketch something out and put it up. The addition was about fourteen by twenty-four. It gave us a new living room, a new kitchen and a dining room. The last bit of building was to fill in an alcove between the A-frame and the addition. There was about an eight-by-ten patio with walls on three sides and we closed it in to create a better place for the kitchen. That would have probably been in the eighties somewhere. My memory is very faulty with regard to dates.

When we first started working on the property we put up an outhouse—the men toted it onto the property from elsewhere—and for the first few years that was our plumbing. Sewage disposal was a challenge on that lot because of the lake and flooding—the septic field had to go away at the back of the property—so we bought an electric composting toilet when they first came out. It wasn't completely satisfactory but it worked. Eventually we got Lawrence to put in a system that pumped the sewage to the high ground at the top end of the property. But even after we got a flush toilet, Al kept using the outhouse. He said it was the source of his inspiration. He kept using it until it became too decrepit. I hear now that there is move afoot to refurbish it.

After we had been there awhile it became obvious that Al needed a place to write. If Jimmy was running around or I was doing housework, he got very frustrated. He used to go into the bedroom where he'd write lying on his side—he always composed in longhand—it looked completely uncomfortable to me but he would keep at it for hours. If we had people over and he

he added on to it to make room for his book collection and about doubled the size. This was Al's private space. I hated to go in the place. It had no windows—there had been one but it got boarded up—and Al would sit in there smoking cigars and writing at all hours of the day and night. It was dark and it stank but he put in more happy hours there than anywhere else.

The final outbuilding we built was the guest house. We needed a place for people to stay, even after the big addition. There were always a lot of people going through. There's a flow back and forth on the 401 between Toronto and Montreal and spots in between and people would just drive in and visit for awhile. We were alone a lot, we didn't have many friends in the neighbourhood except for the old postmaster in Ameliasbugh, so we were usually pleased to have company. Some of the regulars were Rolf and Ruth Harvey and George Galt and his wife, and Milton Acorn. I loved Milton, but you had to make special allowances for him. He was loud and dirty and stayed too long, but his mind was amazing. Tom Marshall had the opposite kind of personality. He had very little conversation. Al was fond of him and missed him a lot after he died, but often

got a sudden urge to write, he would be in pain if he couldn't get away somewhere. So they found a little building that had been chicken coop or something and set that up behind the A-frame, and Al moved in there with his typewriter. Later

44

1. Original A-frame

2. With workroom

3. With new addition and library

4. With new kitchen and library converted to tool storage

Evolution of Purdy A-frame. Drawing by Duncan Patterson.

found him boring when he was around. Tom and David Helwig were in Kingston and both came down a lot with their families. Ron Everson and Lorna were friends for many, many years going back to Montreal. Ron was a lawyer and well off. They had a lovely apartment in Westmount. He was a bit of a square peg in our group, but he was always around the poetry scene. He didn't turn into a great poet or anything but he was one who really kept at it. He had his set time every day when he would go to write. I'm always suspicious of poets who do that because it's contradictory

Left: Kingston poet, critic and novelist Tom Marshall was a fixture at the A-frame before his untimely death in 1993, which struck Al deeply.

Below: Al and Ron Everson ponder flowery subject matter.

to the intuitive part of poetry. How can you sit down and decide you're going to write a poem? To me, and I think to Al certainly, the ideas are there and then he'll sit down. Al would write in the middle of the night if the spirit moved him. Go to sleep, wake up, do a few more lines. If there were people over and he got an idea, he would go off by himself. That was his method. Wait for the idea, but be ready to write when it came. I'm sure he and Ron argued about it—they argued about everything. Ron and Lorna always drove to Belleville or Wellington and stayed in a motel. Our place was too primitive for them. Ron was generous, though. If we went out for dinner he always picked up the tab.

One of our favourite visitors was Janet Lunn, always. We met in Toronto and were friends there for quite a few years and they moved to the county, which was nice. They bought a century-old house, a wonderful old place. We saw a lot of them. Then Dick died and Janet decided to move to Ottawa. She and I still keep in touch. I don't think Irving Layton ever was at the cottage. Frank Scott either. We were not that close to the Scotts. Marian was a well-known painter, he was an important national

Above left: Al with Nova Scotia novelist H. R. (Bill) Percy, one of the A-frame's favourite guests, 1960s.

Al and Eurithe soak up the sun, 1960s.

figure and out of our little social group. We were
a lot younger and not really comfortable with
them. Bill Percy, there was a real connection there.
We met in Ottawa. Bill was a Lt. Commander or
something in the navy and they were running
a poetry series. They got Al down for a reading
so we went down together and as a couple we
meshed really well. They were just such completely
different personalities, Bill and Al. Bill was a little
squirt of a guy with a beard, very laid back, quite
knowledgeable. Vina was wonderful, sort of roly-

Steven Heighton (top, with his family) belonged to a younger
generation of writers who began enjoying the A-frame's fabled
hospitality in the 1980s.

poly with a vibrant personality. They used the
guest house when they visited. As years passed on,
we lost touch with some of our older friends and
younger generations began to take their place. A
young Michael Ondaatje and his wife Kim came
down from their summer place near Kingston,
the poet Michael Holmes came over from Toronto
with Lynn Crosbie, and Steven Heighton and
his young family became regular visitors.

Al liked having people around, but not for
great long periods of time. Of course, there was
many an unplanned overnight stay if they got very
far into Al's wine supply. You'd hardly get in the
door before Al pushed a drink at you. And he kept
on. In the early days, that's what they did. People
would get together and drink, and keep drinking
until they fell down. John Newlove broke his leg
at our house during a night of heavy drinking. Al
would get into some really serious arguments with
people but always connected with drinking. Al was
provocative enough when sober, but provocative
and kind of a bit nasty when he was drinking too
much. But he never acknowledged that, ever.

There were a lot of boozing parties and Al
had good stamina for that but it wouldn't happen
if he was writing. Quite often he'd be working
on one poem for several days and he just had to
keep going. Some of his poems he'd work on for
years. Not continually, but any time he happened
to read the poem he'd find something the matter
with it. Then he'd change it and develop some

Al inspects the charred ruins of the A-frame's garage and guest house that fell victim to an overheated lawnmower.

aspect of it that wasn't coming through at the beginning. He really worked on his poems, although sometimes they came almost full form. I think "Say the Names" was one that came that way. But there were many others through the years. Full form, but still there'd be a word here or a phrase there or something that he'd see on the second or third reading. It's interesting to look at the worksheets and see the little changes that were made. Sometimes Al would read a poem to me and then he'd think, "This isn't right, I want to change it," and he'd change a little bit and he'd read it to me the second time. And I'm still grappling with the first time. And I'm not recognizing the small change. But to him a little change was the difference between good and not good. Many he never was satisfied with. Any scholar who wanted to find out how many hundreds he wrote or started but didn't publish, all they'd have to do is go down to Queen's University and look through his papers. He kept them all.

Before we built the guest house we had no place to put people who stayed over except the loft, and you needed to be part monkey to use that. Mostly people slept on a couch or the floor. Some drove to Belleville to find a hotel. Others camped—I think Sid Marty did that, and Scott

Symons towed in a trailer when he and his very young boyfriend were there, hiding out from both of their families. It was probably the mid-eighties before we got around to building a proper place

for people to over-night. There was a place near the road where the ground dipped down quite sharply so we built a two-level place with a garage on top and rooms underneath. It was very handy, before it burnt down. That happened one year while we were away at the coast. Lawrence and his son had come over to mow the lawn for us and put the mower away in the little place we had for it beside the guest room. For some reason, they threw a blanket over it while the engine was still hot, and after they left it caught fire and burnt the place down. That was the end of our guest room. We took the insurance payout instead of rebuilding. From the practical point of view we should have rebuilt, because we would have got about twice as much and we would have had a much better building. In some ways we weren't very practical people. In other ways, we managed.

As we made improvements the cottage became more liveable but it always remained a warm-weather place. You had to get out before freeze-up or there was no running water. We had a well at first but it wasn't supplying enough water so we used the lake instead. It was very good water. It was a spring-fed lake and we always had the water tested. We got it up to the house with an electric pump that maintained a constant pressure. We still have that. It works fine except you do have to drain it and put it away once the freezing weather sets in. If we didn't get away we'd just disconnect it and get water from the lake by pail, but we didn't stay long when we had to do that. We did spend a few winters in the early years there and Al had to chop through heavy ice to get water. It was most uncomfortable. We had just a wood cookstove for heat and kerosene lamps for light and it took most of Al's time keeping us in wood and water and other essentials. We were so broke we scrounged food from the dump and even ate roadkill. We had Jimmy with us at first, too. He would be about twelve by that time and he and Al didn't get along.

I thought it would be best for everybody to place Jimmy in a boarding school, and took a series of jobs in other places to pay the bills. In

1964 I decided to go back to school and become a teacher, so we moved to Toronto and lived for two years in a quirky apartment in Cabbagetown. Jim was there too, taking a steamfitting course. But right at the time I was finishing teacher's college, *Cariboo Horses* came out and things began to come together for Al. His writing had turned a corner and at age forty-six, having been struggling to write since age thirteen, he suddenly found his mature voice. Again, I marvelled at this. Where did it come from? I think meeting Irving in Montreal, and the other poets down there too, was kind of a turning point. Irving was another guy his own age who was breaking out of the stereotypical poetry of the past—which opened Al up to other things than he'd been doing.

He got a Canada Council grant and we went to Europe. So the year that I should have been teaching, we were travelling. I liked teaching very much but I liked travelling more. It was a choice. It would have tied me down and that didn't seem to be a satisfactory way to live, especially with Al going hither and thither. I enjoyed doing all the bookings and keeping track of everything. I'd been a secretary and it was the normal thing for me to do. Al didn't like being bothered with those things.

It was an interesting life, but we were always looking for sources of money. The publishing of poetry itself is not a lucrative thing, even when you get to the top of the heap. Maybe in some countries where poets are kind of idols it's different, but in Canada a poet just can't live off poetry alone. He's got to be willing to do seminars, to do readings, to do a poet-in-residence if one happens to come up. So we did a lot of travelling and saw a lot of Ontario and other parts of the country, but we were always relieved to get back to the cottage where Al could get some writing done.

People have asked me why we didn't go further and build an all-season home if we were going to stay there so long. I guess the answer is, after those first hard years we got into the habit of going somewhere else for the winter. Our finances improved enough to start spending winters in Mexico, and Florida. Another time we went to the Caribbean and South America. Then from the mid-1980s onward we started living part of the year in BC. I think it was 1985 we stayed at my sister's place in Victoria for part of the winter and the next year we bought our first house in Victoria. So we didn't need an all-season home in Ontario. The cottage suited us. It was still our base and we spent a good part of the year there even though we had a more comfortable home in BC, especially when we got the waterfront place in Sidney. But there's a very different feeling you have about a house when you build it, compared to when you just walk in.

Al always felt stronger roots in Ontario than he did in BC. It's obvious in his writing, really. He got so he could write in BC—he wrote everywhere—but he always did his best work at the cottage. I look through the books now and then. To me it's almost like reading a diary of our lives together. I can't say what my favourite poem would be. Not "At the Quinte Hotel," despite the fact it's had three films made about it. People always want to know which hotel that was, because there were two Quinte Hotels, one in Belleville and one in Trenton. I think he's referring to the one that was in Trenton, which isn't there anymore. Although they boozed quite a bit in both. It's the macho tone of that poem I find off-putting. Al gets branded with that, but he was so much more than that. I like "The Horseman of Agawa." I like the Newfoundland poem. I like the one about the heron—

Stumbling yawning nude to front
Window there on the dock
      In noon fog lit
With his own slow self-strangeness
Stood a tall blue heron

And "Piling Blood," I get chills at times when I read that:

Then at Burns' slaughterhouse
On East Hastings Street I got a part-time job
Shouldering sides of beef…

and I heard the screams
of dying cattle
and I wrote no poems to exclude the screams

which boarded the streetcar
and travelled with me
till I reached home
turned on the record player and faintly
in the last century
heard Beethoven weeping

I always felt that poem expressed a very low point. That's when Al felt that he had to break away— from the work, from Canada, from me. It was just after that he went to France.

There's so many, and they bring back so many memories. If you coupled the published stuff with the poems that are half-finished down at Queen's, you'd have an even more complete picture. Sometimes I feel like going down to Queen's myself.

Often I pick up *Yours, Al* and look at some of the letters. He wrote thousands and thousands of letters, far more than Sam had room for in that book. That is where the real record of our life is, and his personal life. In the fifties and sixties, that was how people communicated. Letter writing was still the thing to do. But with Al it went even further. It was another form of conversation, but much more informative than the actual conversation he had with people. You found out more about Al from his letters than you did in any conversation, I think. He and Margaret Laurence had a wonderful correspondence. I didn't get much out of the correspondence between George Woodcock and Al, though. Too deep for me. I'm

on a practical plane. He never gave up writing letters. Even in the last month or so when he couldn't get to the typewriter he kept writing them in longhand to a few favourite people.

A lot of years together. With some splits. When Al went to France, that was supposed to be a split. It lasted two months or three months, and we were back. Another time when he went to Winnipeg, that was the end. He was out there by himself and I was in Florida by myself. But he came down and spent the break with me, then in the spring we went back to the cottage. Over the years the cottage sort of held our world together.

It was only in the last few years before he died that we pretty much stayed put in Sidney. Since Al died I haven't spent a great deal of time at the cottage. Too many memories. If those walls could talk!

Novelist Margaret Laurence, Al's partner in a long and brilliant correspondence, was an early visitor to the A-frame.

Late Rising at Roblin Lake

Al Purdy

All hours the day begins one may
awake at dawn with bird cries
streaking light to sound to song
to coloured silence wake with
sun stream shuttle threading thru
curtain shadows dazzling eyes at
4 p.m. and 9 p.m. and 1 a.m. one May
awake inside a moving house earthbound
by heart-tick and clock-beat only all
one August afternoon once why
stumbling yawning nude to front
window there on the dock
       in noon fog lit
with his own slow self-strangeness
stood a tall blue heron
            and the day began with him

AL PURDY AT HOME

George Galt

"C'mon down," bellowed the voice on the phone from Ameliasburgh. I'd known Al by mail for a couple of years, not very well, but well enough to call him up and suggest a visit. This was 1978. He had included me in *Storm Warning 2*, one of his anthologies of young poets published two years earlier. So we had corresponded but had never met.

I'd spent about eighteen months recovering from a near-fatal traffic accident in Ottawa, but by this time I had begun to get out, picking up again where my life had screeched to a halt when I'd been hit by a truck. Having missed the launch of the anthology, and missed meeting Al, I wanted finally to talk to this mythical figure who had placed his imprimatur on my work. For years I had been sending my poems to obscure little literary magazines (and occasionally seeing some appear in print). When Al accepted my work for publication by a major book publisher, it was for me a very big thrill.

Al and I had no mutual friends. Working as a bureaucrat in Ottawa, I was part of no literary circle and knew no other writers. So I wasn't sure what to expect when my little Fiat rolled down the dirt driveway to park on the grass in front of the A-frame that spring. I knew from his poems that Al drank beer and wine, so I thought we might have a drink or two, chat a bit, I'd ask him to sign my well-worn copies of his books, and then I'd get back on the road to Ottawa.

What I remember of that afternoon and evening are intense exchanges about Al's and other writers' work, punctuated by the snapping of so many beer caps that I lost count. At one

George Galt, David W. McFadden, and Al (a.k.a. Chelsey Yarn) with the unburnt guest house/garage still standing in the background.

generous hosts. Al became a good friend, but he was much more than that to me. An autodidact with a vast knowledge of books and writers, he became the Canlit professor that I, having studied economics and sociology at university, had never had. In those early years of our friendship he was a mentor to me and a kind of literary godfather, but he offered something else almost as valuable: living proof that it was possible to survive in this country working as a literary writer (not nearly so obvious a reality in the 1970s as it has since become). Summer afternoons and evenings sitting at the Purdy kitchen table overlooking Roblin Lake, trading opinions on and arguing about the relative merits of Frank Scott, Margaret Laurence, Margaret Avison, Leonard Cohen, Irving Layton, Milton Acorn, Margaret Atwood, and other poets and novelists whose books and lives Al had followed closely, this was an essential part of my literary education.

It wasn't quite a classroom, though. In those years Al and I shared a serious interest in alcohol. Booze often fuelled our discussions and the discussions often became high-decibel arguments. At which point Eurithe, trying to read her book in an armchair that was only about ten feet from the kitchen table, would intervene

point near the end of the night I looked out over the Purdys' living room and noted that virtually the entire floor was awash in a small sea of empty brown beer bottles. A drink or two indeed.

At their insistence, I slept on the Purdys' couch that night, as I would on many more visits over the following years. And as on that first visit, Al and Eurithe would always be welcoming and

and order us to pipe down. The A-frame was not quite big enough for two opinionated guys who enjoyed shouting at each other, especially if one of them had Purdy's big baritone voice.

Al was not always a model bourgeois citizen, and he was fortunate to have as a life partner Eurithe, who had in those years a large capacity for near-saintly forbearance. In groups, Al was a mischief maker. Perhaps because he so often felt socially awkward himself, he occasionally liked to be a little outrageous and watch to see who would squirm. Once, when the Purdys were driving my wife and me around the various sections of Prince Edward County—we'd decided to leave Ottawa and look for a country property—Al suddenly suggested we might want to look for a place right in or around Ameliasburgh. "We have a very good postal code," he announced from the back seat in his thundering voice. "K0K 1A0. I think of it as A-1 cock. That's an address that particularly suits me. Don't you think, Eurithe?" What Eurithe thought was that Al was being uncouth. She looked back from the wheel to tell him he was acting like a ten-year-old. And I'm sure that's exactly the kind of response Al was fishing for.

Later the same year, my wife and I bought a stone house on Hay Bay, outside the County, but only about an hour from the Purdys' A-frame. We were distant neighbours for a few years then, going back and forth for meals and talk. Al would bring out the poems that he had been

working on and he would hover while I read them. It fascinated me that this much-admired poet with the big reputation still sought literary reassurance from his friends. He was a vulnerable man, and a remarkably sensitive one. Of course, he was imperfect. He could be overbearing, short-tempered, and egocentric to a fault.

But I've never met anyone else who could hold forth with the rare mix of Dionysian gusto and razor-sharp intelligence that Al brought to our table talk about books and writing. His own best poems are brilliant artifacts that will endure. He was a generous friend and a boon companion.

I miss him still.

The A-frame's living room as it looks today.

Big Al: The Bardic Oenophile and Bacchus, circa 1970

Joe Rosenblatt

Wednesday, October 22, 2008

Dear Reader,

*T*he *Al Purdy A-frame Trust* anthology is a worthy cause, one of the few causes I believe in, among which include the well-being of cats, and lately to my surprise, dogs. Let me start this missive on a Poe trope: It was a dark and snowy night, and animate iridescent snow was piling up in drifts against Al and Eurithe Purdy's A-frame house in Ameliasburg. It was late January, and there I was, the puppified poet, a guest of my mentor, Al, who was about to test my mettle, as to how viscerally serious I was in giving my all to the muse. He was, precisely, inebriated on a thick vino of his own making, redolent of wild berries and grapes matrimonially fermented into a dye that turned the tongue a rich purple, and brought gloss to the eyes. It was in the small hours of morning, when it could be said the ghosts of the early United Empire Loyalist settlers ambulated over the frozen surface of Roblin Lake, a firm snowball's throw from the cottage. I could discern cumulus rising, dense ectoplasmic forms adrift on the lake, sparkling by starlight. I wisely didn't bring that nocturnal mystery to Al's attention, knowing he was devoid of any mystical neutrons, or metaphysical valences, being more attuned to the mundane social interaction and concerns of common humanity, than in the incorporeal-like apparitions.

"You're not fucken committed to poetry are you?" I was taken aback, somewhat rattled by his declarative blast, and intuited that his alien vino was equivalent of a hit of LSD. Al was stoned on his special elixir, a wine that Bacchus would have passed on at a banquet, fearing that to imbibe on that strange potation would be his undoing, and he would topple over on a groaning board filled with smoked venison.

I became apprehensive as any twenty-seven-year-old poetry pup would be in the presence of a huge mastiff, the grand bard fixing his terrible truth-seeking lights on me. The snow was coming down fast and furious, as though the Maker was applying a wicked leaf blower—and the drifts were taking on a life of their own—as an aggregate of crystalline voyeurism. I looked at the increasing increments of snow, wondered if a disagreement with Al on my bardic commitment would lead to an irreconcilable frisson, resulting in my demise under a downy blanket of snow. Faythe couldn't save me, as she had retired to bed at a sensible hour, but not before feeding some logs to the big-bellied stove that miraculously heated the entire house.

"Honest, I am committed," I responded, taking another gulp of his wine, to get hurriedly anaesthetized, for I feared that in his altered state, he might easily strangle me with his pleb weathered hands. A verity voltage, however, on my part, palpably convinced the man I would later call "Big Al" to others, but not in the presence of lanky Al.

"Say, Al, this wine isn't bad. How did you make it?"

He wasn't going to be sidetracked by my query, not in the slightest.

"Look, you got what it takes, but Joe, you can't rely just on inspiration. It takes sweat most of the time, you got to lay your guts out to write poetry."

I nodded in agreement, for I knew the word inspiration an anathema to him, and he would reel up and react like a blinding spitting pit viper on the utterance of the unmentionable—inspiration. Rumour had it that he had decked a few clowns over the over usage of the word. To say that I was a tad scared in my not quite convincing Al that I was going to dedicate the rest of my unnatural life to writing poetry, would have been a mere understatement.

Al had gotten me my first short-term Canada Council grant in poetry, fifteen hundred bucks in 1966, a lot of money then, so I could take time off to indulge my muse, and he wasn't going to see that museful investment pissed away on sloth in producing poetry.

I believe in my old bones that my fearful encounter with Al in those mothy hours changed the course of my creative life. In the years that followed I would have my disagreements with Al, but he remained stoically tolerant when I embarked on my extended exotic zoology—an anthropomorphism—in my endowing bees, bats, fish, cats and other creatures with attributes lacking in humankind. He never understood the nature of my sublime creations and their mythic underpinnings. We were ideologically worlds apart when it came to subject matter in utilizing the power of the muse. He was a poet of state, a

Al Purdy, the dangerous sommelier.

to poetry, he surely must have come to realize that I was hopelessly addicted to the muse—hooked on writing poetry. He could silently respect that.

That A-frame dwelling from my perspective is a temple. Maybe some poet-in-residence will feel a discernable presence in that domicile (perhaps discover a winy stigmata on the pine floor) and then in a verboten freefall of inspiration begin to write reams of memorable poetry, but I ask them to vigilantly look out at that lake for any discernable wintry geists.

Joe Rosenblatt

proud Canadian patriot, who loved the country, its diversity—wrote about the people, even as I lapsed into a subdued obscurity—continuing to invent a bestiary of supra animal beings. My creatures would never darken the gateway of his museful manse, one built on the granite of stark realism. I would like to think that starting from that one bibulous evening, when Al tested my commitment

A-frame 60s Scene

Margaret Atwood

AL PURDY, PHOTOGRAPHED NOVEMBER, 1965

John Reeves

I remember going to Trenton and renting a car, then to Ameliasburg and locating Al Purdy's house. I remember saying "yes" to four fingers of rye presented to me more or less immediately on crossing Al Purdy's threshold. I remember Al Purdy saying something about home-made wine… at just about the time we ran out of rye. I do not remember taking this photograph. It appears that Purdy is sitting on the ground outside his house; the picture propped against his left knee may be a portrait of his wife. Those are obviously grapes heaped on the blanket in the foreground, and I believe that I can confidently assert that the dark fluid in the bottle in front of the grapes is home-made wine. Why am I so confident that that is home-made wine, in what is so obviously a container for Seagram's 83? You may well ask… and I reply: because an identical bottle reposes to this day in my wine cellar filled with a dark red fluid, probably home-made wine. It is my view that I am in possession of an extraordinary CanLit memento—the last bottle of Purdy Rouge Soixante-cinq in existence.

The Winemaker's Beat-étude

Al Purdy

I am picking wild grapes last year
in a field
            dragging down great lianas of vine
tearing at 20 feet of heavy infinite purple
having a veritable tug-o-war with Bacchus
who grins at me delightedly in the high branches
of one of those stepchild appletrees
unloved by anything but tent caterpillars
and ghosts of old settlers
become such strangers here
I am thinking what the grapes are thinking
become part of their purple mentality
that is
          I am satisfied with the sun and
eventual fermenting bubble-talk together
then transformed and glinting with coloured lights in
          a GREAT JEROBOAM
that booms inside from the land beyond the world
In fact
I am satisfied with my own shortcomings letting
myself happen then
                  I'm surrounded by Cows
black and white ones with tails
At first I'm uncertain how to advise them
in mild protest or frank manly invective
then realize that the cows are right
it's me that's the trespasser
                Of course they are curious
perhaps wish to see me perform

I moo off key
I bark like a man
laugh like a dog
and talk like God
hoping
they'll go away so Bacchus and I can get on with it
Then I get logical thinking if there was ever a
feminine principle cows are it and why not but
what would so many females want?
I address them like Brigham Young hastily
"No, that's out! I won't do it!
                    Absolutely not!"
Contentment back among all this femininity
thinking cows are together so much they must be nearly
all lesbians fondling each other's dugs by moonlight why
Sappho's own star-reaching soul shines inward and outward
from the soft Aegean islands in these eyes and
I am dissolved like a salt lick instantly oh
                Sodium chloride!
                Prophylactic acid!
                Gamma particles (in suspension)!
                Aftershave lotion!
                Rubbing alcohol!
                            suddenly
I become the whole damn feminine principle so
happily noticing little tendrils of affection steal
out from each to each unshy honest encompassing
golden calves in Israel and slum babies in Canada and
a millionaire's brat left squalling on the toilet seat in
Rockefeller Center
                Oh my sisters
                I give purple milk!

FROM *A FOOL AND FORTY ACRES*

Geoff Heinricks

And I got interested in the place
I mean what the hell else could I do
Being a little too stupid to ever admit
I was a lousy carpenter and a worse writer?
–Al Purdy, "In Search of Owen Roblin"

At university I was in no way suspected of being an enthusiastic consumer of poetry. A number of friends and acquaintances wrote what I was assured was decent stuff. Then there was Peter Ornshaw—in the intervening years since school reforged as the poet Mountie. Actually, his poems I've always liked and recognized as seriously good things. And yet it never stopped me from appropriating his voice and reciting,

> I think that I
> shall never see
> a rhyming poem
> that's done by me.

To my sensibilities, a lot of what was passed off as poetry reeked of do-it-yourself therapy, though I appreciated that Peter (and a handful of other poets with whom he'd show up at bars in Kingston or Toronto) had something to say, and said it well.

It could have been the instinctual defensive impulse that came of being a high-school kid force-fed the first hothouse growths of CanLit back in the early 1970s. Much of it was of very poor nutritional worth, more the product of novelty and nationalism. Yet I can't gripe. A few things stayed with me.

In grade nine I remember seeing the old NFB film by Donald Brittain about Leonard Cohen, and being impressed—impressed enough to hang out at Ben's in Montreal every chance I got. In high school a few other snippets of the compulsory Canadian content in English classes lodged themselves in my mind too. Margaret

Atwood's disturbing "You fit into me/ like a hook into an eye/ a fish hook/ an open eye" more than made up for spending weeks reading and analyzing *An Edible Woman*. A few other writers also dug themselves into my grey matter. There was something about Hugh Hood's short story "Getting to Williamston" that has stayed with me since grade ten or eleven or whenever it was I read it. Haunted me, actually, though I've never really figured out why. Same as that bit of Atwood.

Al Purdy made more of an impression, but one that lurked below the surface for many years. I'm sure it was discussed in class that Purdy lived in Ameliasburgh, Ontario, an old part of the country, and that it showed in his poems. I can't recall what poems of his we messed with. But I do remember he was one of the editors credited on the cover of the poetry anthology we used at the time.

During a phone conversation with David Carpenter, in the days when there was only the Wicked Point boys, Ed Neuser, Phil Mathewson, and myself, growing grapes out here, he pointed out that the County had a long-forgotten grape history… the same thing Mathewson had mentioned before. And as part of it, surely I had read Purdy's 1968 book of poems, *Wild Grape Wine*?

I hadn't. But I had already begun reading and rereading Purdy poems—the ones in the thick 1986 *Collected Poems* I unearthed one day in one of Toronto's Harbord Avenue bookshops.

Poetry is wasted on people south of their thirties and forties, unless they are poets themselves writing for other poets, reading and warring with each other. I've come to believe this. Either it's a maturity milestone, or it may come from my own pulling back a bit from the modern world… or at least getting my head out of television.

I couldn't find a copy of *Wild Grape Wine* in any of my sweeps through Toronto's used bookstores, so I figured I'd go to the source. Ameliasburgh was just up the road. I knew Purdy collected books, and that authors often accumulated spare copies of their own (especially when allowed to slip out of print) for readings or special sales. Purdy had done just that with *In Search of Owen Roblin*, dropping off a box for sale at the Ameliasburgh Museum. So I wrote the poet and asked if he had a copy he might be willing to sell a County winegrower.

A December morning many weeks later, I pulled out of our post-office box a small envelope speckled in an old, jumpy typewriter face. My name and address were riding high and to the left. The return address ran in a single line across the top: Purdy, 9310 Lochside Dr., Sidney B.C. V8L 1N6.

I had almost forgotten about the query I had sent to him, addressed simply to "Al Purdy, General Delivery, Ameliasburgh." It had eventually reached him… on the other side of the country.

Dear Geoff

sorry, I don't have a copy (extra) of *Wild Grape Wine*. I wish I did have a few copies. Price is up to about $40 these days.

And thanks for the good words re: my stuff. I'm in bad shape right now—pain from arthritis. Taking anti-inflammatory pills et. Tylenol no good at all. I mention this to explain my short letter. It's like a sword, in the mouth and out at the ass. Along the way, it hurts…

A vineyard in Hillier!!! How about all your Presbyterian neighbours?—don't they think wine is wicked? Quakers don't apparently…

Best Wishes,
Al Purdy

I got in touch with him again and asked whether he'd agree to an interview for a piece I wanted to write for *Saturday Night* magazine about his poems on wine and beer and his experiences as a brewer and winemaker. He left an answering machine message saying it'd be fine to come by, now that he and his wife were back in Ameliasburgh. I called and made arrangements to visit.

To help identify the house, on the south shore of Roblin's Lake, about half a dozen miles from our place in Consecon, Al said there was a burnt-out hulk of a garage in front, the result of relatives stowing a still-smouldering blanket they had used to smother a blazing lawn mower. As I walked down the gravel, past the cement-block foundation of the garage, I looked across the complex of board-and-batten buildings, grown from the original A-frame house for which Al and Eurithe used "our last hard-earned buck to buy second-hand lumber/ to build a second-hand house/ …so far from anywhere/ even homing pigeons lost their way."

The tall poet shambled to the door, rumbled a greeting in his unchanging benevolent growl, and apologized for his slightly awkward gait. We settled down at a table in front of a large window overlooking the lake, on a wooden floor salvaged

Al uncharacteristically enjoying fresh air while writing.

from the gym of an old Belleville high school.

I brought out a nice nine-year-old Riesling from the Mosel, and learned something I hadn't expected. The Canadian poet who had written more on creating and consuming wine and beer than probably all the others combined no longer drank.

After some pleasant small talk, he started to speak of his own wines. "I remember taking some to Montreal to Irving Layton's party, and Jack McClelland was there. Jack McClelland claimed it was bad wine. But everybody else drank it. And Jack McClelland, considering his record, would drink almost anything."

I thought that this was a good point at which to open up the Riesling, a pleasant afternoon wine with just 7.5 percent alcohol. Mr. Purdy looked at the label, and grabbed an empty glass for himself.

"Oh yeah. A little bit…That's pretty good. Yeah, that's …I've pretty well sworn off drinking."

"That must be hard for you."

"Yes, as a matter of fact it is. This is a lapse that I hope my wife doesn't see. She went out anyway to do some work in the yard."

"So when did they tell you to stop drinking?"

"Oh, I went pretty near ten years ago to a … specialist—a urologist. He claimed that all the beer I'd drunk in my misspent youth had drowned the nerves. Nerve damage right up to my knees. My legs are clumsy now because of the dead nerves."

From 1957, when Al and Euriche moved across the lake from the village of Ameliasburgh, until 1964, when a young lawyer finally pried Al's inheritance out of the trust company holding onto it, the Purdys lived in dire poverty.

"But hell… when you go through all of this, when you're as broke as all that, it's pretty hard to dramatize," he said, turning to Euriche, who had returned inside. "I was telling him about the time that we were so broke we went over to Mountainview dump and the air force had thrown out all these envelopes of dried—"

"Dehydrated," Euriche said.

"—dehydrated foods. Potatoes, apples, every damned thing. We used them. And we used the paint and the plywood boxes in the house."

"Them were the days," teased Euriche.

"I wouldn't want to go through them again," continued Al. "On the other hand I'm not sorry for having gone through them, because it's all in my own writing and the poems and everywhere else."

"The only thing is, it doesn't do anything for me," added Euriche. "I don't write. So there's no saving element to it at all." She laughed gently.

Al looked at her and said, "In other words, you look back on it in a lot of—"

"Horror," she said, without missing a beat.

"Horror," Al echoed.

This time everyone laughed. Euriche got up and returned to her own tasks.

Al immediately continued, "I don't. I don't, as a matter of fact. It was a hard time. I didn't enjoy it at the time. I was depressed because of it. You can imagine building… we built this house in used lumber. Not all of it. Most of it. Not all of it. This room was built long after.

"I used to chop a hole in the ice. In March it was three feet thick. I'd get out there and I'd sweat so much I'd take off my shirt.

"You go through all this, and you don't enjoy it. But at the same time, it puts you through something, and you get through it and look back on it. I don't regret it a damned bit."

Al paused just for a second, and said, "I've worked when I've had to. And when I got away with not working, why, I did."

Honest words, I thought.

We got back to talking about wine. During the early Ameliasburgh days, Al realized the only way he was going to drink was if he made it himself. "I've forgotten who told me how to make it, but I picked wild grapes. And I picked them in quantity. Real quantity. We had about five garbage pails— seven- or eight-gallon garbage pails—bubbling all at once. And I cleaned them. It was a helluva job!"

▲

After spending a few days in the County, anyone familiar with Purdy's Ameliasburgh poems comes to understand them in a way not possible anywhere else. Live here for a few years, and the landscape rings with his words, not because they impose themselves, but because he's distilled the truths of this place in strings of simple lines.

Even though the poem may be called, "The Country North of Belleville," I can barely look out of the car window in the County without hearing:

> A country of quiescence and still distance
> a lean land
> > not like the fat south
> with inches of black soil on
> > earth's round belly—
> And where the farms are
> > it's as if a man stuck
> both thumbs in the stony earth and pulled
>
> > > it apart
> > > to make room
> enough between the trees
> for a wife
> > and maybe some cows and
> > room for some
> of the more easily kept illusions—

Critics say this may be Purdy's single best poem; read all of it, and I don't believe you'll find a misplaced syllable. Purdy's "Prince Edward County" is not at the same level, though it has some good lines. His numerous others about different pieces of the County shine much brighter.

A prophet is without honour in his own country, proclaim the gospels, and the County is no different from Galilee almost two millennia ago. Purdy is neglected here. The village of Ameliasburgh did name a small lane after him a few years back, but when asked about that, Al usually quoted Thomas Gray's "Elegy Written in a Country Churchyard"—*the paths of glory lead but to the grave*—and then laughed. Purdy Lane is the steep gravel road that ends down at the village cemetery.

Al Purdy's death caught me a bit by surprise. We had drafted him as the Honorary Founding Chairman of the Prince Edward County Winegrowers Association. Eurithe wrote back, accepting on his behalf.

His ashes were to come to the cemetery at the end of Purdy Lane in Ameliasburgh. Filling a rain-soaked day that keeps me out of the vineyard, I drove to Ameliasburgh Museum to buy the last two copies of Purdy's long poem, *In Search of Owen Roblin*. I'd meant to purchase one, but never had the money while I had the thought, and mislaid the thought when my pockets were full; the other was destined for Alberta as a gift to Peter Ormshaw and his wife, Marina Endicott. The books were signed by the author.

Purdy Lane is quite near the museum. Now for some silly reason it is officially called Purdy Street, though a small and weather-beaten hand-routed sign calls it by its earlier name. I walked down its steep drop. A few yards along I could see a wall of wild grapevines. Many

had begun to flower. It was a cheering sight, though I couldn't smell any of that musky, citrusy perfume no matter how close I pressed my nose—it had been washed out of the air.

It was the first time I'd ever explored the lane leading to the mill pond and graveyard. At the base of the escarpment, I wandered into the cemetery and looked over the tombstones, noting many familiar County names on them. There was a fresh foundation for a marker, poured in the last few days. I wondered if this was going to be for

Al, wearing his "Bravo Irving Layton" T-shirt, poses at the local lane named in his honour. The lane leads to the cemetery, causing Purdy to observe, "the paths of glory lead but to the grave."

Purdy. If so, it was nicely sited next to the pond bank. (On a later visit I found that it was indeed his spot.) I wandered back to the gate, and noticed the Roblin family marker. I don't know how I overlooked it coming in. I dropped my gaze and saw I was standing on a small stone nameplate. It said "Owen." I had found him without looking.

Al and Eurithe Purdy moved to Roblin's Lake at around the same age Lauren and I were when we moved to the County, and they had a much harder life than we. As a poet, he didn't really get things going until he was forty. Though our culture only seems to celebrate newness and youth, Al and Eurithe offer a bracing example to everyone who hates their life, finds

it wasted, fears they are failures (as Al said he had felt about his earlier writing efforts).

So many people in their forties rage quietly, internally, against their lives in Toronto or Ottawa or any other city. Most of the people who are planting vines in Prince Edward, or who are looking seriously at land, fall into this demographic slice. The obstacle is always the question of how one survives in the country without two salaries—actually, without any salary. With telecommuting, or the explosion of work to be had in consulting, it is less of a problem than it was in 1957 when Al and Eurithe took off to Ameliasburgh. It can be done, if the passion is there. Al Purdy had the passion to be a better writer. Winegrowing, at least in parts of Europe, is seen as an art form similar to poetry, and it can become a calling many seem to hear but are frightened to acknowledge.

Al Purdy's last poem in his final collection had a few lines that I have taken to heart:

> On a green island in Ontario
> I learned about being human
> built a house and found the woman
> and we shall be there forever
> building a house that is never finished…

Old mill pond, Consecon.

Birds and Beasts

Al Purdy

On the road to Ameliasburg
whippoorwills from nearby woods
sing the very first thought they had
when they first came out of the egg
surprised at being alive
and killdeers run in charcoal dusk
with sparks from the sun's bonfire
while the great black robes of night
slowly lower and lower
Running in front of the car
swerve swerve go little feet
scoot scoot from carbon breath
and roar roar of the Ford beast
home to your nest

Re the whippoorwill:
rumour has it and I would agree
the song actually resembles "More Still"
in the sense of discreet music criticism
instead of the traditional "Poor Will"
whoever that fellow was anyway
i.e. not at all iambic or trochaic
it is like some most enjoyable grief
like the first tears I never let fall
for the first woman I ever loved
when she went away

Poor Newfoundland poor BC and Alberta
they do not go there
mourn ye rugged Newfoundlanders and Albertans
and mourn ye bereft westcoasters likewise
who never hear the bonfire song
the dusk song the heart song of home
And verily be complacent ye effete easterners
for whom the jewelled guts resound
and pour their sorcery in our ears
jug-jug for dirty ears

Nearby they cry "Sleep Well Sleep Well"
to brothers in the woods
and these reply "We Will We Will"
while the little red bonfire dies
and silence   silence falls

THE AL FRAME

George Bowering

Tuesday, May 16, 1967: It was a warm sunny Centenary-year day in what people kept telling me was eastern Ontario. I was driving a maroon Chevy with too many miles on it, on my way from London, Ontario, where I lived at the time in what people told me was western Ontario, though the vast majority of Ontario is west of it, to Montreal, where I would give a poetry reading at a downtown university and, unknown to me, be examined as a candidate for their writer-in-residence job.

I am saying that when I lived in British Columbia, I situated myself by place, its directions and roadways. In Ontario there was no hope of understanding the place. This is so partly because the people there live in history rather than geography. And they tend to mean Ontario when they say Canada. So Al Purdy, we tend to mean Canada when we say Purdy. I turned off the 401, the Macdonald–Cartier Highway (you see what I mean?), looking for the fabled hamlet of Ameliasburgh, or as Al Purdy spelled it, "Ameliasburg," while he was providing its fable. In the Chevy with me were my wife, named Angela, a pain in the ass from Calgary wannabe hippy, whose name was Ron, my Chihuahua dog Frank, and *his* little Chihuahua Small.

Here's what it says in my diary: "On the way up [or down, as it is called there] we stayed overnight at Purdy's famed A-frame house in Ameliasburg, where we had stew and booze and late talk, and in the morning as we were lugging stuff to the car the rural-type assessor arrived as Ron came out with his bells around his neck, and Purdy in his shorts."

An appalling image, but one we all hold dear.

I might have been lost in Ontario, but I knew my way around Al Purdy's poetry in 1967, and I was enjoying myself the way some Wordsworth scholars must feel when they moon over the lake country. There was the church steeple, there was the home-made house, there was the "lake," and there was the wife, Eurithe: "and while that white body protrudes/ over on my side of the bed/ pride is damn difficult …" The little dogs loved it at Roblin Lake, and so did we.

George Bowering photographs Al holding one of the chihuahuas while Angela looks away.

When Angela in her short skirt climbed to look at the loft we would sleep in eventually, Al the perfect host held the ladder and watched to make sure that she didn't slip. When she went to use the outhouse, he manfully flung the door open so I could get a picture for, uh, posterity. She would notice that Al was partly concealed by some leafy branches, and labelled the snap "Al the Faun." In our late-night discussion of poetics, Al said "bullshit" twenty-one times and I said "horseshit" eighteen times. Al was always winning those debates.

In 1967 the Purdys' house was nearly alone on that big pond, and what with old wheelbarrow and upside-down rowboat and empty stubbies in the unshorn grass out front, it all seemed to this innocent westerner a kind of dilapidated eastern elegance, a kind of dogpatch resort, something nicer than I would ever have in my unairconditioned big city apartments. When Al

Al with George Bowering on an early visit to the A-frame.

brought out an old tome full of plot maps for the local Prince Edward County farms given to United Empire Loyalists a century and a half before, he was doing me a favour. Maybe he knew that I was getting to write my book about him—I don't know.

I don't remember how many times I have been to the Al-frame. In the early eighties Brian Fawcett was going to visit Montreal for the first time, so I went along with him to show him around. We turned off the 401 to see whether the Purdys were home, but they must have been in Ecuador or Turkmenistan or some such place, so we just looked around the county, all its old shiny grey wood fences and so on. I noticed that there were a few more houses, or as they call them in Ontario, cottages around Roblin Lake.

Early in the new century Jean Baird and I were driving back south (west) on the 401, after some poetry stuff in Montreal, and halfway between Kingston and Belleville we took a quick glance at each other and smiled, and whoever was driving turned off for Purdy country. Jean Baird and Eurithe Purdy have been comparing notes for years, and on this occasion we got lucky—Eurithe had arrived at the A-frame that very day. I can't remember whether we coaxed her down from the roof, but we sure had a good visit.

I was a little disconcerted to see that the lake is now surrounded by cottages, but that's how Ontario has changed over the past half a century. Grey Owl would have to put up with the generator noise from the next tent if he were schlepping beavers today. But the two energetic Ontario women did have a nice surprise for me. Sometime late in the twentieth century the locals had named a backcountry road for their poet, and Al was amused by the fact that Purdy Lane leads down to the riverside graveyard. That is where Eurithe and Jean took me, to see Al's remarkable headstone, a big black shiny book with the author's name on the spine. What a terrific frame, eh?

Spring Song

Al Purdy

—philosophic musings from under an
old Pontiac while changing the oil
and observing a young lady in summer
attire on her way to the rural mail box—

You neanderthals with guns and bombs
stop exactly where you are
assassins wait in your own dark thoughts
and armies marching thru the rain
with rifles dragging in the mud halt
with one foot raised to take a step
teetering at the dark crossroads
consulting your maps of hell
stop exactly where you are

The world's pain is a little away from here
and the hawk's burst of speed that claws
a fish from its glass house is earlier
and later than now under a rejuvenated
Pontiac with frogs booming temporary
sonatas for mortals and Beethoven
crows thronging the June skies and
            everything still
everything suddenly goddam still
the sun a hovering golden bird
            nothing moves

soft clouds wait
like floating houses in the sky
and the storm beyond the horizon waits
planets stopped in their tracks
high over the village of Ameliasburg
          as if forever was now
and the grass roots knew it all
— but they don't you know and here I am
          with both hands high
under the skirts of the world
trying to figure it out too late for
someone breathed or sighed or spoke
and everything rearranged itself
from is to was the white moon tracks
her silver self across the purple night
replacing time with a celestial
hour glass halfway between a girl
and woman I forgot till she comes jiggling
back from the dark mailbox at last migawd
hosanna in the lowest mons Veneris I
will never get to change the goddam oil

Thinking through an A-frame

Duncan Patterson

The house is an instrument with which to confront the cosmos.
– Gaston Bachelard

Bachelard makes this striking observation in his 1958 book, *The Poetics of Space*. It is there that Bachelard turns his philosophic tools away from science to the study of space, and specifically to revealing those dimensions of space of existential significance, that seem to fundamentally resonate in all of us. But what's interesting is that he doesn't study space directly; instead, he chooses to employ the intuitive apparatus of poets to get closer to his subject, studying Baudelaire, Rilke and Bosco, among others. Poets, he felt, have a privileged perspective. They spend all of their time thinking about dimensions of things that most of us are only barely aware of, and catching them in words. He relies on poets to bring him these things. So what happens, then, when a poet actually builds a house—instead of merely observing space, directly leaves his imprint upon it? How

does the poet's special knowledge affect the way in which he prepares his dwelling place?

The construction of the A-frame seems to have played an important role both in Al Purdy's development as a person and as a poet. Distinguished scholars of Canadian literature Sam Solecki and David Bentley have both commented on it. "I think therefore I am; I think a house, therefore a house is?" wrote Purdy in his autobiography. In laying these two clauses out in parallel, is the implicit conflation of house and self not notable? For Purdy the link between self and house is clearly strong. And for all of us this is true: the making of our houses, whether it takes the form of pouring concrete or banging wood together or of simpler gestures like draping a sweater on the back of a chair, is related to our process of self-making. We are building a frame for our dwelling. The frame will affect how we are

in the house and how we relate to what's outside the house. And Purdy of course knew this, as he gives evidence of in his early poem, "Abstract Plans" (1948), in which he writes of someday building a house, shaping "the windows to watch the road go by,/ with one to catch the starlight and parallel the sky."[1] In this poem the self is clearly positioned in a house, relating through it both to the everyday world and to the infinite.

---

1 Purdy, 'Abstract Plans' in *The Canadian Forum*, Oct. 1948, 160.

1. Between Running and Dwelling

Purdy, who has after all been called both the "first" and the "last" Canadian poet, was of vital importance to the development of English Canadian literature. In the latter half of the 20th century his work was crucial to Canada's developing self-awareness. Dennis

North (lake side) elevation of the Purdy A-frame drawn by Duncan Patterson.

Lee has compared him to Walt Whitman, opening up a space of Canadian dwelling similar to how Whitman had done so in the United States. In Lee's terms, Purdy "placed" us; he "opened room for us to dwell."[2]

Now this is very interesting: when he writes of "opening up," Lee is both echoing the German philosopher Martin Heidegger and also Purdy himself. As Heidegger says in his late essay "Building Dwelling Thinking," drawing on etymology, room, or Raum "means a place that is freed for settlement and lodging." Space, therefore, he says, "is something that has been made room *for*, something that has been freed."[3] Thus, for Heidegger, our very idea of space and room, whether in absolute space or in the abstract space of thought and meaning, bears a residue of the active settling that has made it. He thought of his own work in this way, clearing spaces, what he called wood-paths, for thought.

But Lee's comments, in their evocation of the act of settlement, also echo Purdy himself. Witness the following lines from "The Country North of Belleville" (1965):

> And where the farms are
> it's as if a man stuck
> both thumbs in the stony earth and pulled
> it apart
> to make room
> enough between the trees
> for a wife
> and maybe some cows and
> room for some
> of the more easily kept illusions—[4]

Nostalgia for settler culture held a particular potency for Purdy and in a way he proceeded to re-enact it in his life. It is tempting to agree with Lee when he claims that Purdy performed a sort of secondary exploration of Canada. Slipping into Lee's Heideggerian language we could even agree that while the initial explorers and pioneers charted and settled "earth," Purdy's role was to chart and settle our Canadian "world," an already known and instrumentalized territory, reinterpreted through "poesis."

And in many ways describing Purdy as a "settler" gets at something important lurking beneath the surface both in Purdy's life and his work. A brief sketch of Purdy's life may be useful in understanding why.

Purdy was born in 1918 in United Empire Loyalist country in the town of Wooler, Prince Edward County, in Ontario. The Purdy name had been in the area since the Loyalists escaped the newly confederated states to the south and came to what was then British North America.

2 Lee, "Running and Dwelling: A Homage to Al Purdy" in *Saturday Night*, 87.7, 14.
3 Heidegger, *Basic Writings*, 356, emphasis added.
4 Purdy, *Beyond Remembering*, 79.

His grandfather, Old Rid, a man who occupied a special place in Purdy's imagination, was a rough "lumberjack and backwoods wrestler, barn raiser and don't-give-a-damn-about-anything stud and hellraiser," as Purdy describes in his autobiography.[5] Purdy's father died when he was two years old leaving him to be raised by his mother in Trenton. At the age of seventeen, he dropped out of high school and rode the freight-trains west across the country to Vancouver, which was to be the first of many times that Purdy would cross the country. And here the settler analogy starts to gain some special resonance: throughout the first forty years of his life, Al, first alone and then with his wife Eurithe (whom he married in 1942) and their son Jim, compulsively ran back and forth across the country, like settlers looking for just the right spot.

Of particular interest to Lee in thinking about Purdy and Canadianness was a poem published in 1968 entitled "The Runners." This poem presents a strange sort of settlement narrative depicting the first landing of Europeans in Canada, the Icelandic settlement of Newfoundland. According to lore they had two Gaelic prisoners with them, a man and a woman, who they put ashore upon reaching land. These slaves were instructed to run directly south for a day and a half before turning around and returning with news of what they had found. The poem finds these runners alone in a cold and forbidding place, a place where they cannot settle. But they are also afraid of returning to their masters, so they keep on running, thrown upon this new land but simultaneously alien from it. Lee's thesis is that there is something about this story which is essentially Canadian: "we are half spooked and half at home here… we cannot master the space we have been thrown in, yet are claimed by it and will be home nowhere else."[6] Fair enough. Perhaps we all know something of this tension, but I also can't help but see Al and his wife Eurithe as those two runners in his poem, running across the country from Belleville to Vancouver to Belleville to Vancouver to Montreal to Trenton to Montreal, etc. It's as if they themselves were acting out this tension that Lee describes between belongingness and alienation. I think this tension jumps out even more clearly when "The Runners" is read against "Abstract Plans," published nine years prior to the construction of the A-frame. This second poem begins, "We shall build our cottage where running water gleams,/ And plant the ground with roses and sow the day with dreams," and concludes, "And we shall live forever (a little episode)/ A little past the river, a little down the road."[7] In the time leading up to the construction of the A-frame, Al Purdy seems

---

5 Purdy, *Reaching for the Beaufort Sea*, 16.

6 Lee, "Running and Dwelling: A Homage to Al Purdy" in *Saturday Night*, 87.7, 16.
7 Purdy, 'Abstract Plans' in *The Canadian Forum*, Oct. 1948, 160.

caught between running, like a shivering Gael in Newfoundland, and settling, making Raum for ever, beside the water and "between the trees."

And here we perhaps catch a glimpse of Purdy's poetic knowledge of settling. I don't think it's a stretch to say that we all have some knowledge of this tension between running and dwelling; the poet simply knows it more.

2. Settling

From 1956 to 1957 Al and Eurithe lived in Montreal. In '57, they returned to the Trenton-Belleville area where they had both grown up. As he recounts it in his poetry cycle "In Search of Owen Roblin" (1974):

> I was a failure at writing plays
> a failure at anything in Montreal
> poems plays prose and just being a human being
> which includes everything I can think of
> that was my own situation
> So we built a house, my wife and I
> our house at a backwater puddle of a lake
> near Ameliasburg, Ont. spending
> our last hard-earned buck to buy second-hand lumber
> to build a second-hand house
> and make the down payment on a lot
> so far from anywhere
> even homing pigeons lost their way
> getting back home to nowhere[8]

They settled in a small town south of Trenton called Ameliasburg. They escaped the grimy urbanity of Montreal and Vancouver and returned home. Al's mother was not well, so partially they were moving into the area to be close to her, but there was also an element of escape in their move. Despite Al's claim in his autobiography of feeling like a "sallow-complexioned cigar-puffing expatriate banished from the city,"[9] Eurithe feels that neither of them were ever "large fans of big cities," the country life being really "more natural" to them. And around this time, something in Al Purdy changed. His autobiography is filled with ruminations on why and how people change, astonished at his own transformation that he experienced in the years starting in 1957. As he put it, around this time his poetry took an "abrupt quantum leap,"[10] suddenly maturing, assuming a much stronger, more distinctive voice, a voice both more comfortable and colloquial. As Solecki pointed out in *The Last Canadian Poet*, "in building the cottage [Purdy] began the remaking or reimagining of himself, the record of which is the body of work of the next decade."[11] He built his house, he changed, and his writing changed, simultaneously.

---

8 Purdy, *Beyond Remembering*, 244.
9 Purdy, *Reaching for the Beaufort Sea*, 158.
10 Lee, "The Poetry of Al Purdy", in *Al Purdy: Essays on his Works*, 74.
11 Solecki, *The Last Canadian Poet*, 136.

Interestingly, the site they chose for their new house, in amongst the trees, on the "backwater puddle" called Roblin Lake, faced back north: towards Ameliasburg, towards Trenton, towards the highway, and, through the highway, towards the urbanity that they had left behind in Vancouver and Montreal. It was as if Purdy was removing himself in order to get a better look at things. Symbolically Al seems to have used the property and the building to distance himself from urbane culture and carve out a particular space for himself, with its own particular perspective. And, not unnotably, the voice he was developing in his poetry, with its rather pointed colloquialism, performs a similar sort of trick, carving out a particular space for himself in Canadian literature.

3. Preparing the Land

The property that they chose in Ameliasburg had once been part of a farmer's property that had been subdivided. It was the right price and they knew that they needed to be near water. Initially, they had wanted the land next door because it boasted a spit that projected out into the lake, but they would have had to pay for the extra waterfront. Years later they built their own spit. While they constructed the building they were living with Al's mother twenty minutes' drive away in Trenton, commuting to the site each day. But before they started building

they had to clear the property of the "jungle of willows" that occupied it.[12] As Bentley has pointed out in his essay on Purdy, this sort of pioneering activity seems clearly to mimic Purdy's lumberjack grandfather, Old Rid, in re-enacting "the process of destruction and construction that is settlement."[13] In making "room between the trees" here in Prince Edward County, Purdy was echoing with the sound of his axe not only his grandfather's axe but his great-grandfather's axe too and no doubt his great-great-grandfather's axe as well, clearing both the land and a connection across the generations.

Al describes the preparation of the ground for construction like this:

Early Summer, 1957. Eurithe and I stand near the shores of Roblin Lake. We measure the supposedly equal sides of our house-footing with diagonal lines. That is, we stretch a cord kitty-corner from and to opposite ends of wooden forms. Then we switch sides and do the opposite. This in order that all angles, lengths and widths should match and measure true. All this time, orioles and robins plunge the sun-bright air around us. They build their nest houses in playful joy and love without measuring a damn thing; ourselves in worry and suspense and labour. I grin at the thought, promptly messing up our diagonal measurements, forgetting to keep the lines taut.[14]

12 Purdy, *Reaching for the Beaufort Sea,* 158.
13 Bentley, "A Little North of Where the Cities are," in *Canadian Architexts,* 12.
14 Purdy, *Reaching for the Beaufort Sea,* 162.

It can indeed be said without exaggeration that for Purdy this settling constituted a profound act. It was hardly idyllic, fraught with anxiety and the tensions brought on by the hardiness of the activity and their poverty, but in the end they found some peace in the space they had created by the water. As he writes in "In Search of Owen Roblin," "whatever gods there were/ who permitted pain and defeat/ also allowed brief content."[15]

4. Building

At about the time when they were casting about trying to figure out how to build a house, the June 1957 issue of *Canadian Homes and Gardens* happened to feature a small cottage designed by Toronto architect Leo E. Venchiarutti. It was a recent iteration of the A-frame fad which had been sweeping the United States throughout the '50s.[16] "You can build this cottage for $2000," the cover of the magazine boasted. Within, next to photos of the cottage, the editors offered to send the plans to anyone who wanted them for just twelve dollars. In addition to this notable affordability, due in part to the cheapness of shingles compared to wood cladding, Eurithe says that in selecting these plans both she and Al were attracted to the "openness" of the interior. Right next to the article on the A-frame that had successfully seduced the Purdys was featured an article on a very different sort of cottage: a modernist rectangular box, lifted four feet or so off the ground. In addition to the affordability of the A-frame and its internal openness, it is worth pointing out the difference in sensibility between these two houses. After all, far from floating in the air, an A-frame is a very solid-looking thing, planted firmly on the ground.

And so, with the property bought and the plans in hand, the next piece of the puzzle was to acquire materials, and it just so happened that a large building was being levelled in nearby Belleville at about the time that they were looking to start construction. They were thus able to get a large pile of used building materials for relatively cheap. They carted this material to the building site and started the process of assembling it in an entirely new shape. They "pounded nails/ and sawed boards, cussing and sweating a little."[17] And perhaps, as Purdy recounts, "sometimes all the studding, fibreboard, planks and nails danced in [his] head, like those ephemeral little flies that dance in the bright sunlight," and he "felt dubious about the house ever being built," but, eventually, the house took form, a "ragged cobweb against the sky".[18]

---

15 Purdy, *Beyond Remembering*, 246.
16 Randl, *A-frame*, 10.

17 Purdy, *Beyond Remembering*, 246.
18 Purdy, *Reaching for the Beaufort Sea*, 136.

You Can Build This Cottage For $2,000

Al wrote that they got the idea for the A-frame from *House Beautiful*, no doubt liking the irony, but the more likely source was this June 1957 issue of *Canadian Homes and Gardens*. The A-frame has the same architect as the McMichael Gallery, Leo Venchiarutti.

On the site itself they situated the building just beyond a line of tall cedars and as close to the lake as they dared, given its tendency to flood. The original construction was to be just the seventeen-foot-by-thirty-foot A-frame with a small twelve-foot-square kitchen space off of it. This lasted them through that first winter of 1957–58 although it only had a small wood stove for heat and was more than likely very leaky. But somehow they made it through the cold months alive. Within,

the A-frame was divided into two-thirds to one-third with the two-thirds closest to the shoreline as an open living space with a large window, facing out towards the water, and the remaining third containing the two bedrooms: one for Al and Eurithe and a smaller one for their son, Jim.

A couple of years later Al moved in a small gable-roofed shed and positioned it on the land-side of the building as a place to write. This again engaged in some interesting spatial play with the main building, framing another sitting-space, more open and larger than the one on the other side. Some time around the mid 1970s the Purdys made their largest single alteration in the form of a long, single-storey, flat-roofed, fourteen-foot-by-twenty-eight-foot addition, parallel to the A-frame, on the other side of the twelve-foot-by-twelve-foot structure. This created a small outdoor alcove cradled between the three parts of the house, open only towards the water. This new addition was one single room used as a living room, a kitchen and a dining room. A few years later again, they enclosed the alcove to the north (the one facing the water), and finally made it into a decently sized kitchen.

1. front deck
2. dining room
3. living room
4. kitchen
5. family room
6. hall
7. entrance hall
8. w.c.
9. closet
10. bedroom
11. back deck
12. tool storage
13. workroom

well
lcn

Final floor plan of A-frame and outbuildings and (opposite) elevation of Al's workroom/ library. Drawings by Duncan Patterson.

property line

Al also expanded his writing shack to the south, expanding it three-fold and turning the original part that had been used for writing into his library. Although the library remained without a window, the writing room got one now, but it was a smallish curtained thing that looked back into a small garden. When the garage burned down sometime in the mid 1980s and Al's books were moved to BC in 1987, tools were moved into the room that had been the library and it became a kind of workshop. Though this conversion was primarily the product of contingency, there is something beautiful and worldly about the smooth transition from library to toolshed, and likewise the way in which Al now had to pass through this toolshed in order to reach his writing room, which, fittingly, he referred to as his workroom.[19]

5. Elegiac and Hopeful

The net result of all this is actually quite makeshift, a sort of bricolage of materials cobbled together. Most, if not all, of the materials are reclaimed. There is one place where a metal vent is repurposed as a nailing-plate, holding two pieces of the fascia together, and there is another instance where the writing shack appears to be held up by a bunched-up shingle that has been wedged between it and its poured concrete

foundation. But this is not entirely surprising as his poetry has somewhat the same feel to it. As Bentley has pointed out, many of Purdy's poems can be read as careful compositions of astute literary references,[20] tied together with the bric-a-brac of casual rural Canadian slang. But this colloquial quality was not entirely arbitrary, it served to position Purdy's poetry as a poetry of the people. It glows with a populist ethos and serves as a gesture of reconciliation reaching out to his rural Canadian ancestry, the history of which had already long been threatened with erasure by Canada's rapid growth and change.

For Purdy really seems to have had, in Bentley's words, "a deeply felt sense of pain and loss" in relation to Canada's history. In his

---

19 Purdy, *Beyond Remembering*, 499.

20 Bentley, "A Little North of Where the Cities are," in *Canadian Architexts*, 10.

To make a quiet place to write, Al and the Parkhurst boys trucked in an abandoned shed and set it up on blocks. It's still there, having hatched some of the most celebrated poems in Canadian literature.

poetry, this mourning of the past is evident in such poems as "The Country North of Belleville," and "The Remains of an Indian Village" (1962). But also his desire to connect with this past is revealed in poems like "Roblin's Mill II." In his poetry Al repeatedly returns to descriptions of this old stone mill in Ameliasburg. Through descriptions of this mill, Purdy builds a bridge to the forgotten past. Interestingly, the other primary architectural theme in his poems is the A-frame itself. The first theme is elegiac, the second is hopeful. It is as if in his poetry these two themes are counterparts to each other, the future and the past co-dependent upon one another, the one growing out of the other. As Bentley says, Purdy had a "conception of place as consisting of layers."[21] And in looking deeply at these layers,

as in his poems about the mill, it is as if he could reach back and breathe life into the past.

There is consonance between this thematic project of revitalization and Purdy's use of reclaimed building materials in the actual construction of his frame for dwelling. In the same way that Purdy used his nostalgia and sense of displacement as a lever in his poem-making, Al also employed the remains of fallen buildings in order to construct his own "factual dream of solidity."[22] In his house, Purdy literally connected the old and the new, building the new from the old.

In addition to his themes and in the A-frame, something similar is happening as well in Purdy's use of, to use Lee's phrase, his "hinterland idiom."[23] Poetry can often be written in an inaccessible manner, but the poetry Purdy was now pumping out, especially after the 1950s, had, instead, a distinctively "common-man" feel to it. Often even the metaphors that he chose to employ were very common, such as the wrench thrown into the machinery in his poem "The Machines" of 1962. A man talking in a bar to a friend would never

---

21 Ibid, 4.

22 Purdy, *Reaching for the Beaufort Sea*, 158.
23 Lee, "The Poetry of Al Purdy", in *Al Purdy: Essays on his Works*, 107.

worry that his metaphors were too common; in fact the commonality of metaphors is a great boon to communication. So why, Purdy asserts, should a poet worry about these things? He wants to make a connection between poetry, which he does not want to be elite, and what he saw as every-day life existence, the same instinct which causes him to write in "Place of Fire," "you'll have to admit the ritual significance/ of not being above working with your hands?"[24] Purdy clearly wants poetry to be fully engaged with life as it is commonly lived.

But this colloquialism, the backbone of Purdy's public persona, is especially interesting given that he actually read voraciously. Quite unlike Heidegger who wanted to relate to the sublime landscape when he wrote,[25] Purdy chose to shutter himself into a dark room with his books and his cigars. As Eurithe described to me recently when I was researching this piece, "Al really liked to work in the dark—he didn't want the outside … I couldn't stand to go in there and of course it was always filled with cigar smoke or cigarettes, it would permeate the area." Nothing could be more different from Heidegger's vision of himself as a wise sage sitting out in the landscape,[26] or the stone tower that the poet W.B. Yeats built for himself in Ireland, both of which evoke an elevated sense of mastery over the landscape. Purdy's

A-frame instead seems stubbornly set in the thick of things, with the poet himself cornered up in a dark room with his poetry and his cigarette smoke.

6. (A Little Episode)

Both Al and Eurithe strongly felt the importance of being near water. And, as Eurithe says, it is "kind of a liberating thing for the spirit." It is worth noting that the psychologist Carl Jung also, in building his own house, commented on the need to settle near water.[27] Maybe there is something in a lake's great volume that has a stabilizing effect and offers a sense of permanence. I find some resonance with this interpretation in Purdy's use of water in "Roblin's Mill II" in which he uses the mill pond as a means of moving through time in the poem's narrative, as that which has existed and will continue to exist into the future.[28] The building is oriented, not in conformity to the abstract legal parameters of the space as represented by the road and the property lines, but instead in response to the natural, phenomenal characteristics: past the large cedars, facing towards the centre of the lake. This is very Purdy: non-conformist, attentive to what's important, and obviously water was important.

---

24 Purdy, *Beyond Remembering*, 293.
25 Sharr, *Heidegger's Hut*, 17.
26 Sharr, *Heidegger's Hut*, 76.

27 Jung, *Memories Dreams Reflections*, 223.
28 See Bentley's analysis, "A Little North of Where the Cities are," in *Canadian Architexts*, 10.

"Both Al and Eurithe strongly felt the importance of being near water."

of changing the "contour/ of the earth itself" and "abstracting", fencing in "a portion of the sky."[30] Is this not the poetics of construction? What is it that we do when we build something? Are we not precisely changing the contour of the earth and fencing in the sky? It sounds like hubris, but as a phenomenological description of the building's gathering of space this rings of poetic truth.

As Purdy said in a 1970s' CBC broadcast, the house was to him a "drum for the north wind, a kind of knot in time, tho maybe also a yes,"[31] an insightful evocation of the gathering of time which the structure represents and also the house's engagement with the environment and one that might remind us of another observation of Bachelard's, that "the well-rooted house likes to have a branch that is sensitive to the winds."[32] Built from the bones of fallen buildings, this cobweb of an A-frame, for Purdy at least, tied together the past and the future, the earth and the sky; it was a drum skin between him and the cosmos, with windows to watch the road go by.

So what happens when a poet builds a house? I think it's fair to say that for Purdy the acts of settling the land and building were truly profound, which is attested by the apparent importance they had in his life and in his work. The A-frame gathers both time and space in the form of its structure. Rooted firmly on the ground, it cleaves the sky, bringing the earth up and the sky down. As he says in "One Rural Winter," "the door knob/ is a handle/ I hold onto the sky with."[29] And again in his late poem (1990), "An Arrogance," speaking of the A-frame, he writes,

---

29 Purdy, *Beyond Remembering*, 77.

---

30 Purdy, *Beyond Remembering*, 467.
31 Quoted in Solecki, *The Last Canadian Poet*, 136.
32 Bachelard, *The Poetics of Space*, 52

92

On My Workroom Wall

Al Purdy

Photo of Gabrielle Roy with her much-lived-
in face a relief map with all the wrinkles
like badges of honour
her face a banner in the wind
Two of Margaret Laurence whom I loved dearly
one looking bored the other alight with amusement
Don Coles' poem which says so much about the
lost "Forests of the Medieval World" it loses
me in places I've never been
Harold Ballard on the cover of *Saturday Night*
his cane spanking the world in geriatric rage
My sister-in-law at age twenty-two
so beautiful the photo sizzles despairingly
knowing this one chance was lost
Acorn of course
who dreamed himself into otherwhere
and never found his way home
Me pissing behind the Owen Roblin tombstone
only the stream of piss visible in photo
presaging dry centuries
Poster of Atwood's breasts surmounted by
her Proteus-face which she objected to
or would cancel the reading
Tiff Findley's verse from Euripides
which says "never that which is shall die"
pollyanna stuff but I like it

Eurithe as a fifty-year-old child in water-
colour pretending she isn't there
but she always has been
Xerox of Milosz with cigar looking cynical
Gary Snyder poet-smug and Wm. Everson a dead prophet
Ben Johnson beating Carl Lewis in Rome
grinning back at him like a little boy
saying "Haw-Haw-Haw" without stopping
MacLeish's "You, Andrew Marvell"
—and I too follow shadows around the world
at Petra and Ecbatan and Sumer and Palmyra
and sleep in those ruined cities still
Two original Lawrence letters
both so alive he can't be dead
Three Kipling poems I like much
megaphones into silence
Colour photo: on rock slopes of Nimrud Dag
in Turkey: wrecked stone heads of kings
whose makers placed this glory
atop the mountain
I sit in my rotating office chair and marvel
and wonder that thought itself
could body forth such shapes and forms

I have gathered them all together
like a casual group of strangers
at this meeting place under my roof
who will never meet again
their only relationship supplied by me
who told them to come here
to wait and be silent on my wall
while I contemplate
not their nature but my own
and know as much about myself
by proxy as from looking deep
into the mirror of what I am

It is very puzzling
this flow of self outward
and silent reception in return
and being pinned to a wall
and being what passes for human
and looking again outward
to see myself
a shadow in the sunlight

And Acorn Came with Me to Roblin Lake

Al Purdy

I surprised myself by quitting: the job had suddenly become unbearable to me. This seemed to happen all at once, one day I didn't feel it, and the next day I did. There was a fever in my head to quit that factory. I returned to the house my wife and I had half-built in 1957, leaving her working a nine-to-five job as a secretary in Montreal. I think she agreed that I had to get out of that factory. And Acorn came with me to Roblin Lake.

Several months before this I had applied for a small grant from the Canada Council, with Frank Scott and Layton supplying supporting letters. But that application was irrelevant to my quitting the job: something irrational had stirred in my brain. It said: stop wasting your life conventionally, waste it yourself, unconventionally. And I said: who are you to tell me what to do with my life? (You hafta treat these inner voice know-it-alls as if you have some rights too.) So I went.

The house at Roblin Lake still lacked most of the amenities—even the necessities—when Acorn and I arrived. It was late February, cold cold winter. An ancient wood stove created a small warm spot in the living room, and water would freeze at night a dozen feet from the stove. We went to the frozen lake for water, chopping a funnel-shaped hole in three- and four-foot-thick ice, then scooping water out with a tin dipper. If it stormed between water expeditions, it was very difficult to locate the previous site. The lighting was still coal oil lamps; it's a wonder we didn't go blind.

My brother-in-law Gordon, who worked at the CPR sheds in Belleville, arranged for me to secure a couple boxcar loads of scrap lumber from the railway. I think that wood saved Milton and I from becoming frozen corpses. I managed to borrow an old truck, then Milton and I hauled wood to the lake. Two boxcar loads!—such a huge quantity, it hung around the yard for several years. I used some of it for building a shed, which later became my workroom. We sawed some of our booty to woodstove size with a handsaw, lacking anything better; and just managed to cut enough to feed that ravenous stove and avoid freezing. Much of the wood was Douglas fir and gave an intense resinous heat.

During and between arguments about almost everything, Acorn and I worked at the house. All of Milton's opinions were red-hot gospel. In that cold half-built place—not merely gospel, but Communist Holy Writ direct from the mouth of Jesus-Karl Marx. I really didn't know a damn thing about Communism, but I was forced to learn very quickly. I couldn't let such dogmatism go unchallenged, and scraped the bottom of my brain, desperate for arguments and facts to refute Acorn.

Outside the frozen lake cracked from shore to shore with a sound like God's artillery; inside was nearly as noisy. The moment either Milton or I said anything at all, the other was bound to disagree. And to save my soul and spirit, I had to defend the most ridiculous theories and indefensible positions. What made things more difficult—Milton's arguments were getting to me. I was afraid he'd overwhelm my semantic defences, and I'd accept everything he said in total. I didn't care for that prospect.

But sometimes I was able to see where his skeins of thought were leading, then head

him off at the cerebral pass. Though often he'd corner me with some obscure fact or astute bit of logic which I had entirely neglected. And the arguments continued, sometimes far into the night. The wild grape wine I had brewed in previous years declined noticeably in quantity.

I think Milton took himself more seriously than I took myself—which may have been a good thing, since no one else took either of us seriously. At the end of March there was a literary conference at Queen's University in Kingston, some fifty miles away. Milton

Milton Acorn, Al's friend and frequent verbal sparring partner.

wanted to go in order to escape me; I wanted him to go for the same personal reason. It was getting so we couldn't stand each other. He hitchhiked to Kingston in near-zero weather.

I didn't hear from Milton for three days. I questioned him about it on his return. Too shy to attend the conference, he'd watched writers entering and leaving the university building; ate the sandwiches he'd taken with him; slept on a park bench near Lake Ontario and spoke to no one. He wouldn't actually mention his shyness as the reason he hadn't gone inside the conference building, but his face reddened when we talked about it.

I've seen Milton years later, when some of his shyness was gone, walking across the floor of a crowded room, quite oblivious to where he was and the other people around him. One could say he had spiritual qualities, which sounds ridiculous when you think of that red face and knotted body like an oak branch. But maybe not. Nobody ever thought I was very spiritual either.

In 1962 Milton married Gwen MacEwen. She was very young, wrote poems herself, and appeared rather vulnerable to me. I stood up with them for the marriage at the old Toronto City Hall. After the ceremony they came down to stay with me at Roblin Lake.

This would be in early April 1962. Lake ice had melted along the shoreline, but remained unbroken a few feet away. You could see it under the water. Milton insisted he was going swimming in that cold lake; Gwen and I insisted that he remain on the shore. We told him he'd freeze to death, and he damn near did. Wearing an old pair of swimming trunks and covered with goose pimples, Milton eased his body into the water inch by inch, knowing with every inch he shouldn't oughta done it.

But Milton had a point to make. He'd bragged about being a good swimmer and how healthful cold water was; and a real man from Prince Edward Island would not back away from a little zero degree water in Prince Edward County. Besides, his new wife was there to watch him being heroic—although he didn't mention that. Gwen and I watched the Acorn immersion fascinated, and to some extent enjoying Milton's discomfiture which he couldn't possibly escape by now.

"Warm water, Milt?" I enquired.

He looked at me miserably. "Go away," he said.

Mr. and Mrs. Acorn lived together on Toronto Island for a few months, then the marriage broke up. And Milton came to visit me for consolation. He was helping me with the installation of a television aerial on top of a shed room near the house. We straddled the roof together, one foot on either side of the gable, holding the very heavy aerial at arm's length above our heads. The plan was for both of us to walk slowly toward one end of the roof where the aerial was butted, raising the thing hand over hand, lifting it from horizontal to vertical.

The A-frame aerial, as it looks today.

At the very moment of greatest strain Milton said, "Oh Al, I love her. I love her!" He started to drop the aerial, and it felt like I was holding up the sky alone.

"For god's sake! Milt, hold onto that fuckin aerial, or you'll kill us both!"

And Milton gave the matter some attention.

After a year or two of moping disconsolately between Toronto and Prince Edward Island, Acorn went to Vancouver. He stayed there several years. During that period Gwen MacEwen decided she wanted to get married again, but Milton wouldn't give her a divorce. Gwen asked me to help her, give an affidavit before a lawyer that—in the most delicate terms—her ex-husband had another girlfriend. She told me that no one else would help her, that no one else *could* help her; and she felt desperate.

I pondered over that one long and hard. In the matter of marriage and divorce, I don't believe that either man or woman ought to hold onto the other if they don't want to be held. The feelings between people exist or do not exist, regardless of any law or religious mumbo-jumbo which have no real validity inside a human relationship.

However, my own role in the Acorn/ MacEwen marriage breakup was ambiguous. I was a friend of both of them. In its crudest terms, to supply evidence against Milton resembled a double-cross so closely it made me acutely uncomfortable. But in the end I was responsible for enabling MacEwen to get her divorce.

99

House Guest

Al Purdy

For two months we quarrelled over socialism   poetry   how to boil water
doing the dishes   carpentry   Russian steel production figures and whether
you could believe them and whether Toronto Leafs would take it all
that year and maybe hockey was rather like a good jazz combo
never knowing what came next
Listening
how the new house built with salvaged old lumber
bent a little in the wind and dreamt of the trees it came from
the time it was travelling thru
and the world of snow moving all night in its blowing sleep
while we discussed ultimate responsibility for a pile of dirty dishes
Jews in the Negev   the Bible as mythic literature   Peking Man
and in early morning looking outside to see the pink shapes of wind
printed on snow and a red sun tumbling upward almost touching the house
and fretwork tracks of rabbits outside where the window light had lain
last night an audience
watching in wonderment the odd human argument
that uses words instead of teeth
and got bored and went away
Of course there was wild grape wine and a stove full of Douglas fir
(railway salvage) and lake ice cracking its knuckles in hard Ontario weather
and working with saw and hammer at the house all winter afternoon
disagreeing about how to pound nails
arguing vehemently over how to make good coffee
Marcus Aurelius   Spartacus   Plato and François Villon

And it used to frustrate him terribly
that even when I was wrong he couldn't prove it
and when I agreed with him he was always suspicious
and thought he must be wrong because I said he was right
Every night the house shook from his snoring
a great motor driving us on into daylight
and the vibration was terrible
Every morning I'd get up and say "Look at the nails—
you snored them out half an inch in the night—"
He'd believe me at first and look and get mad and glare
and stare angrily out the window while I watched 10 minutes of irritation
drain from his eyes onto fields and farms and miles and miles of snow
We quarrelled over how dour I was in early morning
and how cheerful he was for counterpoint
and I argued that a million years of evolution
from snarling apeman have to be traversed before noon
and the desirability of murder in a case like his
and whether the Etruscans were really Semites
the Celtic invasion of Britain   European languages   Roman law
we argued about white being white (prove it dammit)   &   cockroaches
bedbugs in Montreal   separatism   Nietzsche
    Iroquois horsebreakers on the prairie
death of the individual and the ultimate destiny of man
and one night we quarrelled over how to cook eggs
In the morning driving to town we hardly spoke
and water poured downhill outside all day for it was spring
when we were gone with frogs mentioning lyrically
Russian steel production figures on Roblin Lake which were almost nil
I left him hitchhiking on #2 Highway to Montreal
and I guess I was wrong about those eggs

From "Al Purdy's Contemporary Pastoral"

D. G. Jones

While every place is a kind of epicentre in the vision of the world as a domestic space, the main centre for Purdy is the A-frame that he and his wife built "with Unemployment Insurance/ and pounded thumbnails" beside Roblin Lake in Ameliasburgh in Prince Edward County in Ontario. The names crop up in poem after poem, and what emerges from these poems is a contemporary version of pastoral.

It is an imperfect Eden of rickety snake fences and abandoned orchards, half wild, half tame, of grass and weeds and the occasional flowers: peonies made to burn against the dull lake water by virtue of five years of fermented garbage, garden fertilizer, and local horseshit. Birds fly in and out and get crushed under cars. Rabbits sometimes dance in the winter moonlight and sometimes end up in the stew. Frogs, "batrachian nightingales," drive Purdy crazy on spring nights, until he goes out in the morning and grabs one, experiencing:

> for this bit of green costume jewellery
> the beginnings of understanding,
> the remoteness of alien love—

Picking wild grapes to make wine, he is surrounded by a herd of cows, like a press of Sapphic maidens; he becomes himself some bovine feminine principle and cries, "O my sisters/ I give purple milk!"

In this "tangential backyard universe," among the transient junk that serves as garden sculpture, Purdy walks with "sidereal aplomb," or wrestles his way to the outhouse, or, grown manic, runs naked into the dew or the snow. Or, at other times, trapped by the cold, with the mice in the walls and the squirrels in the attic, he daydreams

Al with giant tomato plants in his "imperfect Eden of rickety snake fences and abandoned orchards."

of Montreal, the Caribbean, women and sunshine, only to return to the creaking house.

Here he is a somewhat casual husbandman. He moves somewhat warily around the fixed roles of husband and wife, the woman at the centre, who may nurse him through a fever or attack him with the breadknife. Together they may bring the sun and the moon to their bed, or recreate the climate of the Cold War. When she rages or locks him out of the bedroom, he may contemplate leaving her for other women, only to return, in mind as in fact, with mixed motives:

afraid of being
any other woman's man who
might be me
  afraid
the unctuous and uneasy self I glimpse
sometimes might lose my faint and yapping cry for
being anything was never quite what I intended
And you you
  bitch no irritating
questions re love and permanence only
  an unrolling lifetime here
between your rocking thighs and
  the semblance of motion

The family romance is not always idyllic. Relatives may be a pretty mixed bag. The son may be sullen, aggressive, hopelessly incapable of reading Russell or Toynbee, a reminder of age, of Freud, of the Oedipal struggle. Relations in such a household may be mixed, but they are nonetheless personal and particular.

In a poem once cited by a student and which I have been unable to locate since, Purdy tells how one should proceed to build a house: with boards from some old barn, bricks from some old chimney, a door from a house about to be torn down, whatever one can scrounge in the area

that can be reintegrated into a new life and that will integrate one's own life within the local space. According to Lévi-Strauss, this *bricolage* is normal procedure in the development of traditional cultures. It is normal procedure in the development of Purdy's poems.

Generally a Purdy poem focusses on a particular moment, a particular set of relationships, and then it goes round and round like an eddy, gathering up odds and ends, whatever comes to hand, whatever comes to mind, whatever can be caught up and borne along in the current of feeling. It imitates the action of daily life in which one spontaneously digests all kinds of unrelated matters as one moves from situation to situation, moment to moment. It is an action which integrates, not always logically, but sensibly and psychologically, inner and outer space, the local and the cosmic, past and present.

At Roblin Lake

Al Purdy

Did anyone plan this,
set up the co-ordinates
of experiment to bring about
an ecology of near and distant
batrachian nightingales?
– Each with a frog in his throat,
rehearsing the old springtime pap
about the glories of copulation.
If not I'd be obliged if
the accident would unhappen.

The pike and bass are admirably silent
about such things, and keep their
erotic moments *a mensa et toro*
in cold water. After which I suppose
comes the non-judicial separation.
Which makes them somewhat misogynists?
In any case frogs are ignorant
about the delusion and snare women
represent—they brag and boast
epicene, while piscene culture doesn't.

This tangential backyard universe
I inhabit with sidereal aplomb,
tho troubled with midnight debate
by frog theologians, bogged
down in dialectics and original
sin of discursiveness
(the god of boredom at one remove,
discreetly subsidized on wooden plates)—
Next morning I make a shore-capture,
one frog like an emerald breathing,
hold the chill musical anti-body
a moment with breath held,
thinking of spores, spermatozoa, seed,
housed in this cold progenitor,
transmitting to some future species
what the wall said to Belshazzar.
And, wondering at myself, experiencing
for this bit of green costume jewellery
the beginnings of understanding,
the remoteness of alien love—

GRAB A BROOM

Sid Marty

It's May 2008, and I'm rolling into Ameliasburg with poet and film production designer Rolf Harvey, a long-time friend of the Purdys. Eurithe has entrusted Rolf with a key to the A-frame on Roblin Lake. I'd become a less frequent visitor here after the Purdys' move to Sydney, BC, in 1987. They sometimes dropped in at my home in Willow Valley, Alberta, on their annual pilgrimage back east. Those trips ended for Al about 1998.

Ameliasburg's brick and stone emits that immune-to-current-events atmosphere that clings like vines to old Ontario towns, but the Burg has finally caught up with its most famous resident. The local library, home to Al's books and awards, now bears his name, while Al Purdy Street leads down to the little cemetery where our old friend and mentor lies under a big maple tree by the Roblin mill pond.

"Be prepared," warns Rolf, as we turn onto Gibson Road. "It's a bit run down."

Gazing through trees at the glint of lake water, I remember the bunches of wild grapes growing near the end of this road that Al had pointed out to me in the '70s, and savour in my memory the taste of hot, buttered fiddleheads, exotic taste to drylanders like Myrna and I, that we'd picked, fresh, under Eurithe's guidance from her secret field. Once this treed shore held but a cabin or two, a church camp; the feel of isolation still palpable. Now it sprouts second homes, jet skis, boats too big and fast for these meditative waters.

But here is the slanting driveway at number 45, I look hard to see it under the hay meadow of grass that begs to be harvested. The famous A-frame and its flat-roofed addition sit among sprays of lilac still, the barn board siding weathered to grey from the sun and rust coloured where the rain laves it. But the cinderblock garage with the small guest room where Myrna and I stayed in 1986 is but a roofless shell invaded by weeds and bush. It had burned down years ago. Give nature a chance in southern Ontario and she will bury us in jungle.

My sons were still boys on their first visit here. Catching sight of Roblin Lake, they'd exploded out of our jeep with wild whoops, heading straight for the weedy water with a speed and excitement that nearly caused Al to swallow his trademark cigar butt. I don't remember what he said, as he swept his mane of hair back from his forehead with one hand, but it was probably something like

"Holy shit, Myrna! What are you feeding them?" He'd seen their smaller versions in action out west, at least once before. He'd watched, amused, as Myrna ordered them to pitch their tent on the site Eurithe had selected. Al's handshake was both a welcome and a challenge if you were a big guy. He'd beaten me at arm wrestling on at least one occasion. The nature of our relationship? I don't have space to tell much here, but I suppose he was, as he once put it, "a friendly Uncle" to my young poet self, an advisor who became my dear friend.

I gaze from the shell of the garage, to the neglected A-frame, my ears straining for the sound of familiar voices, but Eurithe is in Belleville visiting her son, Jim. She is ill with a respiratory infection, unable to be here with us as planned. Rolf and I exchange rueful glances. The Purdys' absence from this place is a sunset at noon.

Rolf points out how Al's whimsical writing shed, sitting near the front entrance, is slowly sinking into the ground over time. (I wince, because my own writing shack back home is also sinking.) "Nothing in there now but tools and mouse shit," says Rolf. The door is locked, but I peer through the glass into the dim interior, picturing Al's hardwood book shelves—he was so proud of those salvaged OLCB beauties—crammed with books to the gunnels on my last

You can tell it's Al from the tartan shorts and chewed-up cigar.

visit, with barely enough room for his desk, as I recall. (Eurithe and a friend had moved the books to Sydney in 1990—"Some 7–8 thousand," Al had written me—using a 1978 school bus she had purchased from her brother.)

We turned from the office to consider the rotting front deck.

"Shit, we should have brought some tools," I mutter. We are both experienced renovators, but Rolf points out that the foundation has to be rebuilt first. "I worry about Eurithe putting her foot right through it in the meantime, and breaking a leg," he growls.

In we go, a home of rescued, recycled wood, much like my own place, with all the golden hues, the hardwood glows in light flooding through big windows in the addition and in the A-frame. Poets salvaging hardwood, poets salvaging barn board, knowing where to find it, how to save it, where the wild grapes and the fiddleheads grow, knowing how to survive a world that doesn't want you comes easy to some of us. I think it's something we saw in the Purdys and they saw in us, but you'd have to have known poverty on behalf of art to understand it.

The workroom/library/tool shed. Al's original workroom was behind the door on the left, later moved into the shed-roofed addition on the right.

We gaze out through the patio door over the deck Eurithe had built a few years back, to the stony point of land beyond, where Rolf had laboured with Al, Eurithe and Jim to protect the shoreline won back from Roblin Lake. I wrote a song once about drinking a bottle of wild grape wine, then floating it off on a board with a candle burning from that point one night, calling it a concrete poem in motion. I also tried to piss on a star as in a certain famous verse, as a celebration of being there.

Writing this, so far from Ameliasburg, I wish I could describe the chair Al sat in or the table where we'd eaten Eurithe's hot meals on several occasions. I do recall the A-frame ceiling—or was that the wall?—had not been covered with paneling in the '80s, so one could see the insulation through the vapour barrier still. The A-frame felt to me like a summer cottage a young couple had come to, and then forgot to leave when winter came, so they turned the camp into a home, a home, also, for many wandering poets over the years, at least until they got on Al's nerves by interfering with his writing time and were promptly sent packing.

I think we must rescue the A-frame and not let it turn into a mere shrine; it needs human hearts and human voices; it needs the poets it was built to nourish. Al has been well celebrated as one of our greatest poets, but beyond that he and Eurithe were wonderfully generous with their time and with their home. Most of us at some point need the help of a trusted advisor, someone who will demand the best of us without worrying about merely hurting our feelings, just as we need those who love us unconditionally, though sometimes with furrowed brows.

Back outside, Rolf points out the steel TV antennae tower and recalls that a year or so back, some media types came out here and found Eurithe up on the roof, sweeping away fallen leaves. Dead leaves will rot a roof over time. Eurithe had used the tower as a ladder. I gaped at him.

"She climbed up that tower, at her age?"

"She does it all the time, Sid!"

Knowing Eurithe, I don't doubt it, but I think it's time to grab a broom, either literally or metaphorically, and pitch in.

Peonies Beside the Lake

Al Purdy

We fed them potato peelings and rotten meat
we fed them fermented garbage for 5 years
while the stems sickened
        and leaves turned yellow
we fed them garden fertilizer and horseshit
begged from the only farmer with horses for miles
We gave what women have sometimes given
who have no sons and mourn their lost children
        in the menses of growing things
which bear no fruit and cannot be eaten
        except by tongues of the eyes
—or the gentleness of senility in very old women
who really do not know why something aches
inside them when a flower is born
as we are ignorant of our own motives
        after such a long time waiting
to see how the new peonies shine
        reddening the dull lake water

From "On Trying to Wear Al's Shirts"

Steven Heighton

Adapted from a paper delivered May 5, 2006, at the University of Ottawa symposium "Al Purdy: The Ivory Thought." The paper's author did in fact deliver it while wearing a loud blue polyester shirt that had belonged to Purdy.

One afternoon some time in 1983 or '84, Dr. Leslie Monkman of the Queen's University English Department managed to bring both Al Purdy and Earle Birney into our Canadian Literature class for a reading. I was in my early twenties, just beginning to write poetry, and in awe of both poets. Birney, tall and cadaverous, read first, in a croaky voice, ancient and wavering. He read for about twenty minutes and clearly it taxed him. He had a heavy cold. He seemed to grow smaller and more concave as the reading went on. He left immediately afterward on the arm of a beautiful young Asian woman who looked as though she could have been a student in our class.

When Al Purdy got up for his turn and peered down at us, the crown of his head almost grazed the bank of fluorescent tubes on the ceiling, or so it seemed to us—or seems to me now. In a big,

barging voice he prefaced his reading by asking what we had thought of Birney's performance. Nobody spoke. Purdy's high, sunned forehead was stamped with a scowl and his shaded glasses made it hard to decode his expression or even to know exactly where he was looking. After some moments of laden silence I put up my hand and offered that I'd liked the reading, but had hoped Birney would also read from "David," his famous long poem. Purdy stared at me with an unamused grin. A few long moments more and he said, "Yeah, sure, nice old man like that comes here to read, what else are you going to say?" And took the toothpick out of his mouth and launched into a long reading, brilliant and riveting.

If I was surprised that Purdy would crack wise about a fellow poet who'd just left the stage—in fact, an older poet, and one who, I later learned, had influenced and encouraged him—it was because I was naïve then, maybe a bit wilfully, about a natural and unavoidable aspect of the literary world: the competition. Every poet wants to loom tall. Fiercely competitive poets like Al Purdy aim to loom tallest.

I met him and Eurithe Purdy a few years later, at the famous A-frame in Ameliasburgh, in the summer of 1988. He seemed if anything to have grown taller. Over the preceding years I'd gotten to know his poetry well, this process having begun with an essay I wrote about his Arctic poems soon after he and Earle Birney gave that reading at Queen's. Now Tom Marshall and David Helwig had brought me and a couple of other young poets out to meet him. We sat in a circle of chairs on the deck in the sloping afternoon sunlight and we drank beer and talked. David and Al talked, mainly. Al had only a vague memory of his reading at Queen's and when I reminded him of what he'd said about Birney, he smiled wryly as if to suggest, "I don't remember saying it, but it sounds about right."

A scene from the early '90s, one of our by-now annual summer visits to Al and Eurithe Purdy in Ameliasburgh. Al has taken me into his windowless, clammy, mildewed writing shed. It's

above ground but feels like a root-cellar. Still air, muffled sounds. From one of the bookshelves he pulls a slim volume—his first published book, *The Enchanted Echo,* from 1944. "Here, have a look at this poem." Al has shown me *new* work before—and an hour ago, in the house, he showed Tom Marshall and my wife Mary and me a broadsheet that Irving Layton had just sent him from Montreal, then watched us as we read it. You could feel the concentrated, impatient attention behind his dark lenses. I had mixed feelings about Layton's poem and said so,

Old friends, Earle Birney and Al, 1980s.

although I told Al I did like the final image. He seemed irked by this imprudent diplomacy and said, "Aw, hell, I don't think it's any good at all!"

Now, out in Al's creative sanctum, I felt I was being tested again. An awkward moment. These were Al's first published poems. I'd heard he'd disowned them, more or less, but maybe he'd had a change of heart, or had always retained a private affection for the one poem he was now asking me to read. It was clumsily rhymed doggerel, a sort of Edwardian pastiche. I hadn't known Al long enough to be frank. "Well," I said softly, "I think there are some nice sounds in it, but I guess on the whole I prefer your more recent work." Something like that. Al snorted, grabbed the book away and bellowed, "NOW DON'T

Steven Heighton and Al, 1990s.

BE SO GODDAMN MEALY-MOUTHED—IT'S A PIECE OF GODDAMN SHIT!"

Maybe that was the secret of Al's continual improvement. He wasn't just in competition with others, he vied with himself. Was hard on himself. I believe it was Jakov Lind who said that a good writer is somebody who hates himself and loves the world.

I remember saying to Eurithe Purdy, shortly after Al's death, that I thought Al was a man who had always taken death very personally. And she said, "Yes, I think that's true." I will add that I think his life's work in poetry was a way of talking back to death, to time and gravity—the gradual attrition of the flesh. In fact Al *competed* with death—not just with other poets, mentors, and himself. I sense that for him this vying with death was the ultimate competition. And the beautiful fuel of his poems.

Al's best poems, I think, are unbeaten—or, as the saying goes, they *stand up*. Maybe I'm just making a case here for aesthetic emulation, since the competitive urge is dangerous to a poet's growth only when its object is status rather than achievement. And the two things are not the same. They rarely equate as they ought to.

The media (for instance) will never care much about actual achievement—only about status and rank, hype and buzz, scandals and angles.

It's utterly natural but slowly damaging to yearn for plaudits another poet has enjoyed; on the other hand, it's utterly natural but aesthetically *healthy* to read a good poem and then set out to write one as good, or better. It was the second of those urges, I think, that most drove Al's writing.

▲

Why wear the shirts of a mentor poet if one's goal is not to write poems like his? My own poetry is increasingly different from the work of this poet I've learned from. So? I wear this shirt because it was a sort of deathbed gift, much as

Al's mentorship was a gift to me. So this shirt embodies the support and encouragement he gave. I wear this shirt because it's my connection to a mentor who understood that I not only loved his best work but envied it, vied with it, took inspiration from the challenge of trying to stand equally tall. I wear this shirt because it's a reminder of all that can't be kept but must be passed on. And to be part of a tradition. And, to be sure, out of love.

And I always envied Al his shirts.

Steven Heighton with family and friends, and Al and Eurithe (centre), on an annual summer visit to the A-frame.

Al's Outhouse

Seymour Mayne

It was its own almost leaning
                         tower
of Pisa
     though many a Can. Lit.
Kilroy
      honoured
that bagel-shaped seat
     with an obligatory balanced
squat
     hoping to keep it
                  from tipping.

"Make sure you sign
             somewhere on the wall!"
Al bellowed
      and I wondered
where better should this privy
be propped up
         than in front
of the National Library,
            a monument
to the literary cadres
        adding their contribution
to the pit
      before lime burning time
erased the inspired droppings
           of generations.

From *A Trip Around Lake Ontario*

David W. McFadden

Everybody thought it was a good idea to phone Chesley Yarn, the most famous of all Canadian poets (you should read him if you already haven't). He didn't betray the spirit of poetry by setting out on a big vulgar campaign to make himself famous. He just became famous naturally, because his poems were so good. We were all hanging around the general store in Carrying Place, eating sticks of licorice and trying to not look too much like tourists. We talked about it quite a bit and decided if there were tourists driving through they would probably think we'd been living in Carrying Place all our lives. There was a phone booth.

Yarn was a great old guy who drank a lot of hard liquor, and when he visited you he wouldn't leave until there wasn't a drop left. He'd wiped me out booze-wise a lot of times. It's true, there were four of us that day, but altogether we wouldn't drink half as much as Chesley. We wouldn't shout and carry on as much as Chesley either, and we wouldn't argue with him much. I felt sorry for him living way out in the sticks and trying to be a great poet. He had a wonderful wife, but still aside from her there wasn't much input. He didn't seem to need it though. The greats never do. They are the input. Like Mozart. It comes from God. Via the songbirds of the great forests of our youth.

When I phoned him he told me to get there right away. I said there were four of us, "Geez-us, are you ever in luck," he said. "Elsie just put on a pot of spaghetti big enough to feed an army. Bring a case of beer, will you?"

"Uh, how do we get there?" I'd been there once before, with my ex-wife before we were married, when we were still high-school sweethearts, more than twenty years ago. I wanted to be a real poet just like him, and wrote and told him. I sent him some of my poems that had been cruelly rejected by the high-school yearbook. He thought the poems were terrific. He told me to come and visit him and he'd give me some tips about how to be a real live poet like him. I couldn't believe my luck. I was dying to meet a real live poet.

"You continue along the highway towards Picton, and you come to two signs. Take the second sign, it's just past the big house on the right, a green sign, make a left turn and go right down the road for seven miles. There are one two three four five turns, go past the village, straight through, to one mile down the road then turn left. You come to a dead end. We are the one two three fourth house down the road, there's a big double garage. A big blue roof—on the house, not the garage. It's an A-frame. Got that?"

I told him I thought so and asked how his arthritis was coming along. He laughed and snorted, happy I'd remembered, "It's all right. I'm mobile. I just bought a new car. Yeah, a brand-new Mercury."

"Nothing like a new car to make you forget your arthritis."

"Right."

He said he wanted to put us all up for the night. The three guys in the spare room and me in the library. "And have you got anything to drink?"

"You already mentioned that, Chesley. You told me to bring a bottle of beer."

"A bottle?!!!!"

"No, I mean a case, sorry."

"Kee-rist."

Chesley Yarn was dressed in a clean white polyester dress shirt, sleeveless, the top three buttons undone, and a pair of bell-bottom checked trousers with extra-wide cuffs. A postcard was sticking out of his shirt pocket as if begging to be noticed. Yarn had grown a nice grey moustache since I saw him last, and was chewing gum. There's a saying in California: "You can always tell a Canadian, they wear checked pants and chew gum."

When I came to a halt right next to Yarn and flicked off the ignition he held out his hand as if to shake mine but when I extended my hand he shot his long thin knobby leathery arm past mine, grabbed the case of beer sitting on the passenger's seat, ripped it open, pulled out a beer, twisted off the cap and took a big slug, all with one hand. It was a joke, it was serious, it was getting dark.

A lot of people, even people who admired Yarn's poetry, found him a little hard to take in the flesh with his loud voice, checked pants and country manner. There's no doubt he had a tendency to be obnoxious and belligerent and he certainly had a tendency to clean out your liquor cabinet before you could think to lock it up but to me he was fascinating because he was a natural, that is I was always trying to discover something phony about him but never could. He wasn't playing the role of the hard-drinking loudmouth poet, he simply was a hard-drinking loudmouth poet.

All we did was guzzle beer, eat huge platefuls of spaghetti (as soon as you'd finish one plate Elsie would grab it and place a full one back down in front of you) and argue about writing and writers. I hadn't been involved in a conversation like this in years, it was embarrassing, indecent. I felt a touch of culture shock, but I plunged in and maybe even was the worst offender, arguing, gossiping, cajoling, pretending I'd read books I hadn't.

Now and then Elsie would gently lose patience and ask if we might change the subject and we tried to but it never lasted long.

Eric was talking about his trip to the University of Western Ontario library archives where he was looking through the Yarn holdings and found a letter Yarn wrote in 1967 when he was mad as hell at somebody or another. "Oh yeah, I remember that," Chesley would say, and he'd be off on some bizarre string of gossipy anecdote designed to make himself look good, and it seemed funny and entertaining, especially when we all weren't talking at the same time as was often the case…

I incautiously suggested that Yarn might take a look at the later poetry of William Carlos Williams because Yarn was almost the age Williams was when he suddenly blossomed and began writing the greatest poetry of his life, but I quit when Yarn said he'd never taken an interest in Williams because his old friend Louis Dudek had always been trying too hard to push Williams on to him. "I don't think Williams was interesting before he was sixty-five," said Yarn. "I think you have to be interesting both before and after you get old."

"Listen carefully, Yarn," I said, "I have been privately predicting for years that you were going to write the best poetry of your life in your old age, and now here you are almost elderly. What do you think?"

He heard me and blinked, flattered. "What can I say? You're scaring the shit out of me. But I do think my best book was my last book, the best I ever wrote, but that's just my own opinion."

I guess a lot of the time I was trying to get the conversation settled down and serious, but come to think of it we all seemed to want to do that at different times, and each time one would try the other two would panic and change the subject or make some goofy remark.

"It's important to talk about these things. There's nothing more important than poetry," I said. Everyone agreed.

"What were we talking about?"

"Poets suddenly changing, making big breakthroughs, as I have been predicting will happen to Yarn in his old age and I hope it does because then when I get to be old I'll have his great poetry of maturity to read and to inspire me."

"People like me who live a long time as apparently I have seldom grow and change," Yarn looked sad.

"Maybe none of us ever really change, but Williams' poetry certainly changed, after he had that stroke."

"Look, I went through a period of ten years when I didn't grow and change at all and I hardly even knew it. I was just content with myself." Yarn then began professing, as he often did, that he knew nothing about poetry. "If I knew how to write poetry I would do it all the time. I have no idea. I don't know fuck all about fuck all."

Eric was talking about his book of collected or selected reviews that had just appeared, with a blurb by none other than Chesley Yarn on the back cover, and it was something Chesley was claiming he had never said, it was a misunderstanding on the part of the editor. Something about Eric's criticism reminding him of D.H. Lawrence's. I mentioned I'd just been reading Lawrence. Eric said I looked like Lawrence. I said I hoped I was healthier.

Eric made a comment on *Sons and Lovers* I won't repeat.

Chesley started quoting lines from Lawrence's poetry. Something about delighting in the companionship of fire, a companionship more naked and interpenetrating than love. "Sheer genius," he said. "Anyone who could say that in a poem is a pure genius."

Eric agreed, as he agreed with all Yarn's opinions.

We argued about what critics were worth reading (I was pounced on viciously for calling George Woodcock a hack), and we argued about Ezra Pound and Herman Melville and Rilke some more and William Carlos Williams. We even got into some weird kind of spat about Paul Theroux, and at that point Elsie broke in again, this time in an even sterner tone.

"Isn't there something else to talk about beside writers and writing?" she said.

"Yes, what about this movie you're making?" said Chesley.

"Well," said Nigel, "we're going to come back in a couple of weeks and do some more shooting after Captain Colourful here finishes the book."

"It's gonna take him longer than two weeks to finish the book, isn't it?"

Yarn just really wanted to tell Nigel how to make a film. Not that Yarn knew anything about film, but it couldn't be that much different than writing a poem could it? If you can write a poem you can certainly make a film.

DAVID W. MCFADDEN

"Just let yourself go," he said. "Don't worry too much about the subject, indulge your sudden rushes of genius, otherwise you're doomed because your basic material is so… well…" He eyed me meaningfully. I was listening, waiting for the word. He wasn't going to say it.

"Scintillating?" I said. Laughter.

"One of the nicest things about this trip so far," said Nigel, "was…"

Yarn wouldn't let him finish. "I would have thought you arriving here was the nicest thing so far," he said, "I really think it's nice you came." I suddenly noticed his moustache. Had he had one before?

"Did you just grow the moustache recently?" I said.

"No, I've had it for quite a while."

"Why did you grow it?" I was serious and curious.

"Ah, we're all trying to escape anonymity," he said.

And so Eric wanted to know why I had a beard and so on. Chesley wanted to know about my kids. I brought him up to date, and mentioned that my older daughter had just graduated from nursing college and the younger was studying photography. I happened to mention the older was short, only five feet even.

"Do you want her to be tall?"

"She says when you're tall people expect more of you."

"Is that true, Eric?" asked Chesley.

"I'm not tall, ask yourself."

"Nobody ever ever ever expected much of Chesley," said Elsie, who was washing the dishes.

"I bumped into the ceiling yesterday, changing a light," said Eric.

I said I'd never bumped into a ceiling in my life but I'd bumped into a few floors.

"It's not how high you are it's hi how are you," said Rodney. Everyone laughed.

"Now," said Elsie, "do the non-beer drinkers want coffee?"

I told them the story about the kids saying we like your car, Mr. McFadden. Eric accused me of having made the story up, but Elsie appreciated it. "That would be a bit unnerving, I would think," she said.

Chesley brightened up considerably, "No, it's not un-Irving," he said. He'd had this postcard in his shirt pocket ever since we arrived and was continually pulling it out, fiddling with it, then putting it back in. It was obviously something he wanted to share with us and now he had the chance. "Speaking of Irving, I have a postcard I want to read to you. I don't think there's enough light to get it on camera." Hint hint.

Nigel sprang into action. "We can light it up pretty good," he said.

The postcard was from the famous Canadian poet Irving Layton and was in his famous patented insulting style: "Dear Chesley: You miserable cretinous parochial Canucky schumuck." Apparently

Layton was annoyed because some of Yarn's letters had just been published, and Yarn in a letter about twenty years ago had said something unkind about Layton, that he'd never write another masterpiece. "I want you to know I went on writing masterpiece after masterpiece, only to put ulcers in your fat gut and haemhorroids on your fat stinking ass. So, in spite of your awful limitations, you're an authentic poet and I take my hat off to you. Your last book moved me as few books had. Your friend Irving.

"Hah haw," said Yarn, who seemed to be the only one impressed. "Your friend Irving. Isn't that something? It's typical of Layton that he tears you down then builds you up. Oh well, what can one say about Layton?"

Nobody said anything, not even Eric. We all looked bored silly.

Nigel backed off.

"There's coffee here for anyone who wants it," said Elsie, again with perfect timing.

Nigel and the guys wanted to leave. They didn't want to stay over. They had to get a motel so they could do their inventory for U.S. Customs. We figured we'd be crossing into the States early the next evening. We agreed to look for each other the next day at two in the lobby of the Holiday Inn right on the Rideau Canal waterfront in Kingston.

Yarn became very sweet. "We should give them a sandwich to take along. It would of course be a spaghetti sandwich."

"No, it's okay," said Nigel. He started mumbling to himself. We were standing outside in rural starlight, a little additional light coming from the house and faintly but charmingly from the town across the lake.

Winston was just standing there looking sleepy and content in the soft Southern Ontario autumn starlight. Yarn turned to him and asked him where he was from. He hadn't said much all night, just listened, occasionally chatting with Rodney.

"From Toronto," said Winston. "English background, actually. Lived in Yorkshire for a few years."

"None of us can help that," said Yarn.

"You mean our backgrounds?"

"Exactly."

"Where are you from?"

"Oh well, from this area. Not here. Trenton, born north of Trenton. But that's irrelevant as you know. What you are is a whole lot more important…"

"Than where you're from?"

"Well, it's wrapped up in it of course." Yarn was suddenly quietening down and becoming peaceful and wise. He must have been tired.

"But you can turn out all sorts of different ways," said Winston.

"Oh, yeah, all sorts of different ways… Oh well, I'm gonna drink the rest of the beer. Nice meeting you."

News Reports at Ameliasburg

Al Purdy

In the night of my sleep at embassies
in Hong Kong and Cairo and humid oil capitals
of Arab republics in New York and Moscow
in London and Paris in Accra and Rome
the people say no
philosophers search for new absolutes
hopheads pry into their negative psyches
Bedouins march thru stoplights of sand dunes
pickets circle round factories with banners
black non-violence reaches invisible barriers
at houses abandoned by wealthy distillers
rocks break the glass and death discolours the gutters
battalions of students are shouting their slogans
and the centuries roll onward like mass-produced coffins
to carry the world wherever the world may be going

At Delphi the Oracle gives odds on war and Leonidas
turns aside from the pass at Thermopylae
to attack the Americans
Hannibal drives his elephants into Toronto
Cleopatra and Antony have signed a treaty with Caesar
to burn down Chicago and destroy Los Angeles studios
Alexander turns from the gates of the Ganges
and moves with his generals and phalanx to bulldoze the Kremlin
while the eunuch priests conspire in Assyria
to defoliate the Vietnamese rice fields of bananas
At night in our own bodies comes a small dark whisper

relayed here from the beginning of human time
where ancient hunters confer with stones and tree-spirits
their campfires throwing enormous shadows on the forest
and witch-doctors dance in our blood forever

Only behind the centuries is something near silence
before the glaciers turned into ice cubes
before there was man
no young students to ponder old questions
of right and wrong and be sure that life is no bargain
but more important than sleep is
the windows are breaking around me

The groundhog pushes a stone to the mouth of his burrow
the goldfinch repairs his nest with a patchwork of sunset
the fox removes his teeth to a glass for safekeeping
squirrels retire to a rotten tree and the damn thing blossoms
pike in the monocle eye of the lake have switched off the planets
I have unbuckled my sword and lie there beside them
the sun has gone down in my village.

The Woman on the Shore

Al Purdy

A music no Heifetz or Paganini knew
it never occurred to them there could be
—at night when man-sounds fade
and shadows pretend to be shadows
the lake is trying to decide about itself
whether it is better to be ice or water
and can't make up its mind
it yearns toward both of them
And little two-inch tubular crystals form
phantoms in the water
—when the merest hint of wind comes
they *sing*
they sing like nothing here on earth
nothing here on earth resembles this
this inhuman yearning for something other
sighing between the planets

On earth
I have manoeuvred myself near them
my face close to the crystal hexagons
kneeling uncomfortably
on this rocky shoreline near Ameliasburg
temperature 32 degrees Fahrenheit
shining my flashlight on them
trying to observe the exact instant
water stops being water
becomes uncertain about what it is
trembling
it shivers and questions itself until
until the ice-amoeba in the world's veins
sings in midnight silence

I can't stand the cold
run back into the house to escape it
you watching at the window
questioning me:
"What happened out there?"
—kneeling on the rocky headland
remembering something left behind
shivering a little in the bedroom
my cold hexagons and your warm flesh
refusing to come together
and the cry of one lost animal
wandering the frozen shoreline
wanting to be everything
and silence
and sleep

Maybe I Said Something that Annoyed Newlove

Al Purdy

I met John Newlove nearly thirty years ago, at Binky Mark's annual party in Vancouver. Binky was a short plump man with liver lips and a sort of overproof complexion, a well-loved character in lotusland for no reason I ever discovered. He worked at Duthie's bookstore, and seemed to know everybody and everything. Before joining Duthie's he ran a leftist bookstore near Hastings Street. Customers entering the place were said to be photographed by the RCMP, on the grounds that anyone entering such a crummy establishment must be Communists.

Anyway, Binky's party, and everyone who could rhyme moon/June or spell freeloader was there. I ran into Newlove just after memorizing where Binky had hidden the beer with commendable foresight. John was drinking rye and grumbling that he couldn't get any beer himself. I procured one for him, and with my usual tact and diplomacy knocked the rye glass out of his hand while handing him the desired brew. Newlove immediately tried to kick me in the balls, my evasive tactics narrowly successful. I could see that we were meant to be friends for life.

Without a place to sleep that night, Newlove invited me to occupy his quarters while he bunked with friends. It was a good arrangement, I thought, since the hour was late and I would've had to convince a hotel desk clerk of my complete sobriety.

However, the room was located right in the middle of a pottery factory—at least that's what it looked like to me. A kind of oasis, separate from all the dust and working clutter. And more, the place was directly under the Granville Street bridge. Traffic roar kept me awake for much of the night. I think the only reason Newlove was able to sleep there was he stayed sloshed most of the time. When I woke up early Sunday morning and opened the door to the factory proper, the

John Newlove.

first thing I saw was a torn-apart copy of *Slava Bohu*, a book about BC Doukhobors, on a nearby bench. It was a library copy. And I could see that John had a proper respect for literature.

Newlove showed up before noon, and dug out his poems for me to read. I thought they were pretty good, and also felt obligated

because of the free room. I took the manuscript back east with me, giving it to Peter Miller at Contact Press. Later on, this manuscript was the basis for Newlove's book, *Moving in Alone*.

Over the years John has been a combative character. If we were friends part of the time, we were enemies for the rest. On one occasion at George Jonas's apartment in Toronto, we both had our fists cocked at the ready, confronting each other like over-age roosters. But John blinked first, on accounta he had to pick up a beer with the hand he generally used to grow a left hook. I can't remember what that one was all about.

Newlove was always broke or nearly so; conversely, he was always able to find money to buy booze. It has never been quite clear in my mind how we became friends, a relationship which he would deny vehemently.

One occasion with John and I drinking beer remains crystal clear to my mind and blurred at the same time. This contradiction calls for an explanation, since I'm confused about the incident myself. It was about twenty years ago. John was an editor at McClelland & Stewart then, and came to visit Eurithe and I at Ameliasburgh. Ron Everson and his wife Lorna were also guests at the time. And beer was available in some quantity, both John and I sampling it to the extent that only samples remained.

It was after midnight, that I do remember. We were in the kitchen, and everyone else had

gone to bed, as sober and sensible people are wont to do. John and I were talking, of course, perhaps even arguing. My own sensitive nature generally precludes argument, but in this case the provocation was considerable. And a pause ensued, although I am not sure what it ensued after—I mean what event took place just before the pause. That event, whatever it was, resulted in John and I being washed toward the kitchen door, propelled there by a huge wave of water. I felt complete bewilderment at that instant. Danger of drowning wiped everything else out of my mind.

Of course we grabbed the doorsill while passing, and thus saved ourselves. Eurithe then emerged from the bedroom to ask in a sarcastic voice for the reason we were washing the floor at this time of night. An answer seemed uncalled for.

Next day I spent some time trying to figure out what happened, reconstructing the order of events in reverse. John and I had been standing by the kitchen sink, that much was certain. That

The kitchen, somewhat altered from the time when hard-drinking poet John Newlove mysteriously broke his leg in the middle of the night.

sink had a sort of overhang built-in at floor level, enabling your feet to slide under and the dishwasher could stand close to the job. Since the water pump wasn't working, we had a ten-gallon plastic can of water placed nearby. We'd overturned it somehow. I think John must've had his feet trapped under that sink overhang, and when we fell had preceded me toward the floor, knocking over the water on his way down. But why did we fall in the first place?

I can't remember, and beyond the point of forgetfulness I don't much want to remember. But I am curious. Maybe I said something that annoyed Newlove. Maybe I said pleadingly, "I didn't mean to insult you, John. I apologize if I did." Maybe he punched me or I punched him. Cross-examination in a court of law might result in illumination but enough said.

Next morning John had a sprained foot, and couldn't walk on it. Since we intended to visit our friends, Angus and Barbara Mowat, at Northport that afternoon, I was forced to become a beast of burden. Not without a few words of protest either. I slung the cripple over my shoulder, staggering around the backyard a few paces while Newlove screamed in my ear. John had started to eat heavily since achieving lucrative employment in Toronto, while continuing to drink just as much as ever. His disposition didn't improve either. He weighed nearly 200 pounds.

That ankle got more painful through the day, and finally I drove Newlove to Belleville hospital. I was getting pretty worn-out by this time anyway, whispering to Eurithe, "Don't give him anything more to eat; he's breaking my back already."

As it turned out, John had a broken ankle. He had to be fitted with a pair of crutches in order to get back to Toronto a couple of days later. The medicos in Toronto inserted a pin in his ankle-bone. And the moral of the lesson is—keep your temper. At least I think that's what it teaches.

I haven't seen Newlove for years. According to my information, John Metcalf's wife got him a job writing Mulroney's speeches in Ottawa (if it was me writing those speeches Mulroney would have been fired a lot sooner than he did). That job paid sixty-five thousand a year some time back, which probably ensures plenty of brew at John's right and left hands. And I've had a bad back ever since that visit by John Newlove.

THE YEARS

David Helwig

It was in 1970 that I made my first visit to the A-frame Al and Eurithe Purdy had built themselves in 1957 on the flat, grassy shore of Roblin Lake. You drove down the main street of the village of Ameliasburgh—A-burg as Al always called it in letters—past the octagonal house, the church with its slim shining spire, and then you turned left and went round the end of the lake, left again to their driveway. And left once again into it. The house was isolated in the early days, though as the years went by more and more of the lots nearby were sold and houses or cottages built. Since the choice of urinals in those days was between an outhouse and a not-very-efficient chemical toilet, a multitude of visiting poets pissed on the back lawn. I once swam naked off the little dock beyond the young weeping willows.

In September of 1970, Tom Marshall and I drove down from Kingston and spent the afternoon and evening with Al and Eurithe. At the time I was in the middle of marital problems, and the two of them were kind about my precarious emotional state. Al played a couple of his favourite recordings, Burns' "Ae Fond Kiss," Kenneth McKellar singing about the Bonny Earl of Moray. I wrote about it later.

> I sit in the almost silence
> listening to the scrape
> of pens, read undeceived
> terrible words on the nature
> of love and remember
> the gentle soaring
> of the song of Burns
> you played for me,
> a song about the parting
> of man and woman
> and the accepting of it.

Al told me how he and Eurithe had once separated but ended up back together again.

> And there are times when stew
> or beer or a soft boiled egg
> or the voice of Gigli, rain
> and morning, waking in my clothes
> in a strange room make a better story
> than he said and she said and then …

On that first visit, Tom and I stayed over, sleeping in the loft of the A-frame.

> And now there is this poem,
> a kind of memory, a kind
> of thinking, hearing
> an old Scotch tune, this poem,
> a kind of thanks.

Later in the autumn I made the trip again, with Tom and some other friends including Don Bailey, someone I'd first met when I was teaching in Collins Bay Penitentiary. That visit was the occasion when Don managed to fall into the water-filled hole that had been dug for the foundation of a new kitchen that was to be added to the house. That kind of thing happened in those days.

Writers were always turning up at the Ameliasburgh house. You heard anecdotes—how Scott Symons' lover was frightened of Al and wouldn't leave the trailer they'd parked out the back and come into the house. Al was affectionate and hospitable toward his literary visitors, but he never presented himself as a candidate for sainthood. There was the story of John Newlove's mysterious broken ankle, how late one boozy night at Ameliasburgh a great flood occurred in the kitchen and Newlove fell victim to it. Al told the story as if it was all some kind of divine mystery. Now Newlove is dead, maybe no one will ever know exactly what happened. Though he

was a loyal friend—witness his long devotion to Milton Acorn and his poetry—Al was capable of anger and a malicious wit. There was the summer afternoon at Ameliasburgh when the name of an Important Canadian Poet came up. Call him X.

"I like X," Tom Marshall said in his kindly way.

"We all like X," Al roared. "And we all wish he was a better poet."

The Purdys seemed prepared to welcome any number of guests, though Al could be prickly with those who rubbed him the wrong way. On one occasion a young man and his girl who lived somewhere nearby arrived while I was there. The citified young literary man was wearing old-fashioned farmers' overalls, and Al was determined to provoke a fight between the two lovers about the odd outfit. Worked hard at it. Some days Eurithe was absent with the car, doing errands, or now and then looking at properties; she had a weakness for real estate. Eurithe was a teetotaler, and I remember at least one occasion when she walked into the house, looked around, and said in a steely voice, "Well, what time did the drinking start today?"

For all his enjoyment of his role as barroom brawler, and his occasional childlike need to be the centre of attention, Al had a fierce alertness. He didn't miss anything. You'd be sitting in front of the A-frame on the shore of Roblin Lake and find that he was hearing more than you intended

to say. Or later on it would turn out he'd been watching when you hadn't guessed he was.

I visited Ameliasburgh on and off over thirty years. The house was expanded to include a new dining area with an adjacent living room. Out the back they built a one-room shed in which Al worked, and where he stored his large library of Canadian books. He once showed me a copy of the poems of Louis Riel which he'd picked up in his travels. The house grew more accommodating as the years

---

Al with Tom Marshall and students. The A-frame was that very rare sort of place a lit prof could take his students to visit a famous writer at work, then get invited to stay on for dinner.

passed, the trees on the lot grew tall. More neighbours built houses and cottages. Eventually Al spent only the summer months there.

My visits to A-burg over those years were most often with Tom Marshall—me driving because Tom didn't. After Tom's sudden death, I was the one who called Al at Ameliasburgh to give him the news. He was fond of Tom, tolerant of his eccentricities, and I knew he'd want to be told. When I said the words, he wasn't silent or sad or thoughtful as most might be. He shouted—and it was loud—just one word, "No!" I remember the first trip to his place afterward, scarcely out of the car and sitting down when Al said, "Well, I guess we're here to talk about Tom."

What Al cared about most was poetry. When you arrived at the A-frame by the flat little lake he'd pull out a poem he'd just written, or somebody's poem he'd just read, demanding to know what you thought of it.

I remember an occasion when he quoted some new lines he'd just come up with. "And death, the idea we are used to/ like a far away train wreck." He tried the lines in one or two poems, but I think it was only years later that they found their final home.

He liked complications—not easy paradoxes, but the two sides of things being lived out at once. "I can be two men if I have to," one poem says. "For being anything at all was never quite what I intended," says another one. His vision, even when he wasn't making jokes, was essentially comic because he saw more than one thing at a time. Some part of the secret of the best poems is this doubleness, the immense presence of the man, the largeness of the space he took up, alongside a capacity to see the other aspect of things "there by indirection," to look back from around the corner, to be in the present, the past and the future all at one time. The timeless kept intruding on the ordinary.

I was once on hand while it was happening. In the 1990s, a group of us who had driven down from Kingston were sitting around at Roblin Lake, about to eat a lunch that Eurithe had prepared. Al was playing a favourite record of the German baritone, Erich Kunz. The song he was singing, *Muss i denn,* had the same tune as that old Elvis Presley hit, "Wooden Heart." I started to sing along, the English words. That's what took place. That's all. Did I look at Al and notice something? Did Steven Heighton who was sitting nearby? Should we have known that Al was in the grip of something mysterious? In the poem, published in *To Paris Never Again*, that event, the song in two languages, became one of those Purdy moments of entrancement—

a full six seconds removed
from the texture of time
not recorded by clocks
the world rotating without us …

And later:

> —during that lost time
> old kingdoms have gone to ruin
> fragments of silence
> trapped in crumbling walls
> and time enough for wind
> to pause and whisper
> a secret to the river
> something about
> a water nymph
> who was once human
> and time enough
> for every secret
> to be forgotten

There we all were, just waiting for lunch, when that vision occurred. Or at least the intuition that led to it. Or was it, maybe, only afterward that Al remembered that moment and thought of its doubleness, thought of how two realities, two languages, were claiming the world at the same time?

It was the summer of 1999 the last time I saw him. We were staying at my old house on Wolfe Island, where Al and Eurithe had visited a year or so before on one of their trips to Kingston. I knew about the cancer—that surgeons planned to remove it but found it was too large. Time was running out. We drove from Kingston to Ameliasburgh and sat in the big living room for as long as Al could manage. Then, tired out, he went to lie down. What did we talk about that day? I'm not certain. Poetry I assume. Over the next months we sent letters, his written by hand, since the pain in his shoulder made him unable to type. He hung on until the next spring.

Al died in British Columbia, but his ashes, all that was left of him contained in a surprisingly small wooden box, were buried in a quiet cemetery at the edge of the mill pond in Ameliasburgh, the site of Owen Roblin's mill, which turned up in so many poems. It was a simple ceremony on a bright summer afternoon, and many of those present dropped handfuls of earth into the grave. He was buried under tall green trees by poets, Margaret Atwood and Michael Ondaatje and Susan Musgrave and the rest of us who were there. In the middle of one of the short speeches, six Canada geese came swimming down the mill pond, looked things over, spread their big wings and flew away.

One Rural Winter

Al Purdy

Trapped
        abandoned
        marooned
like a city thief in a country jail
bitching about all the fresh air
the rural mail my only communication with outside
surrounded by nothing
        but beautiful trees
        and I hate beautiful trees
I'm lost beyond even the remote boundaries
of Ameliasburg
        and I ask you
what could be more remote than a burg
named after a German dumpling named Amelia?
Why just close your eyes tight shut here
and you don't see little dots of light
        —you see fresh cowpads
But it's winter now
        beyond the economic wall
(I have two nickels a dime and quarter
and not a damn cent
in my pockets but a wife
who comes out at night when I'm asleep
and won't meet the burning stare
of my closed dreaming womanless eyes
not for two nickels a dime and quarter anyway)

Al Purdy

        In the backyard
phallic pieces of wood and stones embedded
in ice (notice the Freudian terminology please)
a failed writer I'm trapped forever
in the 3rd Post-Atomic Pre-Literate Glacial Period
(making witty remarks like "Cold out, ain't it Zeke?")
It's got so I'm even afraid to go outside
in order to experience the rich rural experience
that is part of our common Canadian heritage
I might catch my foot in a lateral moraine or something
and be trapped forever
        in Ameliasburg Township

The earth is frozen
the beautiful trees are frozen
even the mailbox's metal nose is cold
and I'm getting a little chilly myself
living in a house I built one tropical summer
with Unemployment Insurance money
        and a bad-tempered wife
But I got into this mess myself
and I ain't blamin the Class Struggle
besides things are gonna get better
in ten or twenty years I think

It does improve my character
        no doubt of that
to walk half a mile to the outdoor shithouse
with the temperature at 40 below
But *Maclean's* Magazine is absorbing toilet tissue
and all the spiders and microbes and things

I trained last summer to sit up and chant
in unison Hallelujah What a Bum
      to visiting imaginary females
from the neighbouring seminary
      —are frozen stiff
But the place is warm and comfortable
despite the perfumed gale below
as long as you can keep your mind
      on the beautiful girl
tacked on the wall who advises that
      SPRING IS HERE
and I should have my crankcase flushed out
Then wiped and buttoned and zippered
I plunge back to the house
thru a white world of nothing
      but snow
      and the damn WIND
steals all my internal heat
it howls like a dog in my summer underwear
my heavy body is doped with wind and cold
      and the house door
      drags me into the hall
      and the door knob
      is a handle
I hold onto the sky with

Remembering Al

Janet Lunn

In the weeks since Al died, friends, newspaper columnists and fellow poets have written about his importance to Canadian poetry, to Canadian culture, to Canadian identity. His fellow poets will probably talk more about that today. I want to talk for a few minutes about Al as a friend.

He was as awkward with his friendships as he was as a public figure. Because he was such a self conscious person, he seldom noticed how other people felt so he could walk all over your feelings, and then if you turned on him, hurt—or rageful—he'd be astonished. As for being perfectly oblivious to the fact that he was boring you, well, as someone pointed out in one of the post-mortem newspaper articles, Al would shove one of those boring—though, quite likely, valuable—books he'd bought for trading purposes, and insist on telling you all about it even after you'd shouted in his ear, "I don't care about this book, Al."

His enthusiasms were as big and powerful as he was. Like tidal waves, they engulfed everyone near him. He loved to eat mangoes. He bought them in fat bunches and I hardly ever left Al and Eurithe's house without being given a mango to take home. He loved hockey and would insist on describing the details of an elaborate play to me even though he knew I had neither interest in or knowledge of the game. He loved to read aloud the poetry of D.H. Lawrence and play records of Paul Robeson and the Soviet Army Chorus singing as loudly as his record player would play. How often I've had those bass Russian voices singing *Kalyinka* chasing around in my head, days after an evening at Purdys' because Al had wanted to hear it over and over and over again. He'd dance around the room—well, maybe not exactly dance, it was more like leaping—wildly directing the choir with his arms and demanding of everyone in the room, "Isn't that wonderful!"

You had to agree with him—not only about music, about everything—or you were in for an argument. And Al loved to argue! I remember evenings over dinner in the cottage when he would say one outrageous thing after another just to get us going. Then he would rock back on his chair and laugh and his laughter

Al and Tom Marshall being themselves.

would spur him on to say something even more outrageous. Then he'd say something he thought was very funny and, if Eurithe or I—or both—wouldn't laugh because we didn't think it was all that funny, he'd carefully explain it.

Often he *was* funny, of course. He had a wry, puckish sense of humour and a lovely, contagious chuckle. And he did love to tease. Few opportunities to get a kick out of a situation

140

passed him by. I don't think I'll ever forget the summer afternoon I stopped by the cottage to find Al and Milton Acorn sitting out on the back deck. I had never met Acorn and, while I'd read some of his poetry, I didn't know his views on a lot of things, not his obsessive anti-abortion views, anyway. Al either knew or suspected this so, as soon as I'd got myself nicely settled, he introduced the subject of abortion. Acorn started in to rant. I was quick to respond. Al left. It wasn't more than two minutes before I noticed, by the flick of a curtain, that he was watching through the window, a huge grin on his face.

On the other hand, times when I was sick, when my husband was diagnosed with cancer, when there was a serious problem with one of my children or a close friend, Al would phone to commiserate. "That's awful!" he'd say and then he'd start talking about something else because that was really all he could think of to say in sympathy. But I always came away from the phone feeling comforted.

He was like this with all his friends. He could bait unmercifully, tease endlessly, then say something or do something to show how much he cared. But he seldom realized, himself, how much he cared and he was surprised when he found out. I remember how upset he was when Tom Marshall died.

"Tom was so quiet," he said. "Such a quiet man. You'd kinda forget about him. Didn't know how much I liked him. You don't notice those quiet people until they're gone, do you?"

Over the years since then, he often talked about Tom and how much he missed him. And every time it seemed to surprise him. He was like that when Bill Percy died, too. When Al found out that Bill was so ill, he had a hard time taking it in. "He's such a sweet guy," he said and it embarrassed him to say it. "I guess you shouldn't say a man is sweet, but damn it, Bill is!" He shrugged his shoulders uncomfortably, trying to slough off the sentiment but he couldn't, he cared too much. When Bill died, Al felt the loss terribly and he didn't really know how to handle it.

In these last years he worried a lot about Eurithe. After Al and Eurithe moved to Sidney for their winters, Al always came back to Ontario a month early in the spring (Eurithe stayed behind to take care of things in Sidney). We got into the habit of going out for Sunday evening supper together. "She's been up on the roof again," he'd say, the worry thick in his voice. "She shouldn't do that. She's had a heart attack." But, then, almost in spite of himself, he'd smile and shake his head, "She's amazing, you know, she's really amazing."

The thing is, that under the gruff awkwardness, Al, too, was "a sweet guy." He *was* a large presence—and he was an endearing presence. He's left an awful hole in the place where he used to be and I expect all of us, we who loved him, are not yet quite sure how to walk around that hole.

Because We Were Poets

Michael Ondaatje

We were very young and he was hitting his stride—*Poems for All the Annettes, The Cariboo Horses.* There had been no poetry like it yet in this country. Souster and Acorn were similar, had prepared the way, but here was a voice with a "strolling" not "dancing" gait or metre, climbing over old fences in Cashel township… (And who ever wrote about "township lines" in poems before Al did?)

And with this art of walking he covered greater distances, more haphazardly, and with more intricacy. Cashel and Ameliasburg and Elzevir and Weslemkoon are names we can now put on a literary map alongside the Mississippi and The Strand. For a person of my generation, Al Purdy's poems mapped and named the landscape of Ontario, just as Leonard Cohen did with Montreal and its surroundings in *The Favourite Game.*

We were in our twenties (and I speak for my friends Tom Marshall and David Helwig, who were there with me) and we didn't have a single book to our names; we were studying or teaching at the university in Kingston.

… And Al and Eurithe simply invited us in. And why? Because we were poets! Not well-known writers or newspaper celebrities. Did Kipling ever do that?

Did D.H. Lawrence? Malcolm Lowry had done that for "Al—something or other" in Dollarton, years earlier.

These visits became essential to our lives. We weren't there for gossip, certainly not to discuss royalties and publishers. We were there to talk about poetry. Read poems aloud. Argue over them. Complain about prosody. We were there to listen to a recording he had of "The Bonnie Earl of Murray." And sometimes we saw Al's growing collection of signed books by other Canadian poets. (My favourite dedication among them was "To Awful Al from Perfect Peggy.")

All this changed our lives. It allowed us to take poetry seriously. This happened with and to numerous other young poets all over the country, right until the last days of Al Purdy's life. He wasn't just a "sensitive" man, he was a generous man.

Al and Eurithe entertain a youthful Michael Ondaatje. Some people may have left the A-frame mad but nobody ever left hungry.

Most of all we should celebrate his fervent, dogmatic desire to write poetry. A glass-blower makes money. A worm-picker has a more steady income. Al, a man who had the looks and manner of a brawler, wanted to be a poet. And what is great is that he was a bad poet for a long time and that didn't stop him. That's where the heroism comes in.

And when he became a good, and then a great poet, he never forgot the significance and importance of those bad poets—they were rather like those small homes and farms north of Belleville, "a little adjacent to where the world is," and about to sink into the earth. He had been there. It gave his work a central core of humbleness, strange word for Al. It resulted in the double take in his work, the point where he corrects himself.

"I have been stupid in a poem…"

As he was not ashamed to whisper in a poem—this in a time of mid-century bards. Al never came with bardic trappings.

"Who is he like?" you ask yourself. And in Canada there is no one.

I can't think of a single parallel in English literature. It almost seems a joke to attempt that. He was this self-taught poet from up the road. What a brave wonder.

So how do we respond to all that Al was and stood for?

The great Scottish poet Hugh MacDiarmid, who was pretty close to Al in some ways, had by the time of his death become the embodiment of what his country's culture was, and stood for, and stood against. Fellow Scottish poet Norman MacCaig recognized MacDiarmid's contribution by saying:

"Because of his death, this country should observe two minutes of pandemonium."

If You're Ever Down My Way, Drop in and Say Hello

Paul Vermeersch

The first time I was invited to the Purdy A-frame was in March of 1995. I was a student at the University of Western Ontario, and one of my professors was Stan Dragland, who at the time was moonlighting as the poetry editor for McClelland & Stewart. Purdy's latest collection was *Naked with Summer in Your Mouth*; it had just come out with M&S the previous fall, and I knew that Stan had worked on it with Purdy. When I mentioned to Stan that I was a fan of Purdy's work, without hesitation he said, "Well, you should write to him and tell him yourself," and he wrote down the address for me on a scrap of paper.

So I wrote to Purdy, and along with my earnest letter of praise and deference I included some dreadful piece of juvenilia meant as a tribute to the master. Purdy soon replied—which for some reason surprised me—and in his reply he offered his telephone number and an open invitation to visit the A-frame in Ameliasburg whenever I was able. The famous house! It figured in so many of his poems, I felt I knew it. He also encouraged me in my literary pursuits, but cautioned me that poetry was hard work and told me I had a lot of work to do. He was right, of course, but I was glad to be told so by someone I admired so much.

That letter was as precious to me as oxygen, and I kept it neatly folded in its envelope in the front of my copy of *Naked with Summer in Your Mouth* for several weeks until I framed it, but I didn't make any immediate plans to pay my poetic hero a visit in his fabled Prince Edward County home. I didn't want to overdo it, wear out my welcome when it had only just been extended. For the time being, it was enough that he had written back, that he had encouraged me in my writing, and that the invitation to visit had been extended at all. The visit itself could wait.

We exchanged more letters and occasionally bumped into one another at poetry readings and festivals. I remember a time in Toronto in the spring of 1998 when Purdy was reading with Dennis Lee at the Imperial Library Pub, and later that year I ran into Purdy again at the Eden Mills Writers' Festival. He kept repeating the invitation: "If you're ever down my way, drop in and say hello."

"I will, Al, one of these days. I swear." I suppose I was just waiting for a more convenient time.

Sometime in late 1999 or early 2000 at some book launch in Toronto—I can't remember which one, and truth be told, it hardly matters now—a mutual friend pulled me aside and whispered into my ear that Al had been diagnosed with lung cancer, that it was very serious, and that Al was dying. I stood there stunned and pale and bleary eyed for several minutes. Someone asked if I was all right. "I just found out that someone is dying," I said. Then I left my drink on the bar and went home.

It's easy to forget that poets like Al Purdy only have a claim to immortality in the metaphorical sense. To me, he was a giant of a man, both physically and poetically, and even though he was already past the age of eighty, it never occurred to me that he might die anytime soon. With a younger man's selfishness my thoughts turned to Ameliasburg and the invitation to visit the A-frame. I had always supposed that I had all the time in the world; it was an open invitation, after all; I would get around to it. But that grim news whispered to me among the throng of oblivious party-goers was like a sudden jolt, the realization that important things will not always wait, that there may never be any such thing as a more convenient time. Purdy was dying. He would write no more poems. He would encourage no more aspiring poets, at least not in person. No one else would ever be able take him up on his generous offers to visit him in his famous little hand-built house.

That I had five years to accept that offer and never did was, and always will be, one of my life's great regrets.

I did get to the A-frame eventually. The day Al's ashes were buried in Ameliasburg, Dennis Lee and his wife Susan Perly were kind enough to offer me a ride in their car. By mid-morning, I was there: the A-frame. Finally, I was paying my promised visit and at the same time paying my final respects. The house was filled with relatives, friends and neighbours, and many members of Canada's literary establishment, along with a smattering of younger writers, including myself, who had benefited from Purdy's legendary generosity.

There were even more mourners, roughly two hundred in all, gathered in the little cemetery in Ameliasburg, at the end of Purdy Lane. I remember feeling a little star-struck by some of the "big names" in attendance. I quickly found my head, though, and committed my attention to the occasion of the day. There was a modest graveside service, nothing too religious for Purdy the atheist, but spiritual enough for the faithful among the mourners. Some solemn remarks were made, but the bulk of the eulogies would be delivered later on in Ameliasburg's town hall just up the road.

When the official talking was done, everyone milled about the gravestones, reminiscing. For some, it became a game to spot unusual things etched on the marble and granite monuments: a motorcycle, a German shepherd, a half-ton pickup truck. Like the Pharaohs of Egypt, the people of Ameliasburg were buried with images of the things they loved. Fitting, then, that Purdy's stone is book-shaped. Not wanting to lose sight of my ride home, I stood by the gravesite with Dennis and Susan who were chatting with Margaret Atwood and Graeme Gibson. The day was wearing on, and there were still many eulogies to be given. Eventually it was Atwood who said, "Well, perhaps we should get going, then." And so we got going.

The five of us were the first to leave the cemetery and make our way along Ameliasburg's main road back to the town hall where the rest of the eulogies would be given. And that's when something marvellous happened. Across from

Eurithe Purdy in June, 2008, at Al's book-shaped gravestone, which she designed with Rick Van Krugel.

the town hall there was a house, and on the lawn of that house there was a yard sale. Rows of picnic tables were set up, and they were cluttered with decades of accumulated treasures: fishing poles with missing reels, a plastic roadside mailbox shaped like a cob of corn, boxes of old records and old books, crates of dishes and various utensils, many of them never used and never to be used, a tea cozy shaped like a chicken covered in crocheted posies. Again, it was Atwood who spoke. "I think Al would have stopped here," she said. And so we stopped.

When I looked back down the road, the crowd was beginning to file out of the cemetery and make their way toward us. As they approached, it seemed that everyone noticed us checking out the tables at the yard sale, and one by one, they joined in. Soon, the yard sale was overrun with an unexpected (though I imagine welcome) two hundred visitors from the cemetery. Being a perfect occasion to pick up a souvenir from Ameliasburg, almost everybody bought something. I remember Dennis and Susan bought some folk art: a pair of animal figurines made of seashells glued together with large googly-eyes. Lynn Crosbie bought a drinking glass that had, for no reason anyone could discern, actor Jamie Farr's face etched onto it. And someone else bought the plastic corncob mailbox.

By the time people had taken their seats in the town hall, the place was filled with junk from across the street. The fishing poles leaned against the wall next to a pair of badly beaten cross-country skis. One woman sat with a fourteen-inch black-and-white Zenith TV set on her lap. Some of the more serious readers in the room were comparing books they'd found: a book-club edition of an Ian Fleming novel and a cookbook specializing in wild game. So filled was the hall with the genuine ephemera of Ameliasburg, it was as though some unwritten Purdy poem had come to life to remind us not to take matters too seriously. In fact, Purdy's memorial was suddenly furnished with odds and ends and snippets and scraps of every imaginable origin, much like, it should be noted, the materials that composed his hand-built A-frame home.

The presence of all these souvenirs cast a decidedly lighter tone over the rest of the day. The eulogies were delivered, by writers and friends and family, and the mood was now more celebratory than mournful. I had purchased an unused notebook at the yard sale, and I had resolved to write a poem of tribute to Al in it, a better one than the one I'd sent to him in 1995, but I left the notebook on the floor underneath my chair, and the appropriate words for such a tribute poem, one worthy of its subject, have still not come to me. At least, not yet.

Al standing at the gate to the place where the words come from.

The Al Purdy A-frame Trust wants to preserve the Purdy house in Ameliasburg as a lasting reminder of Al Purdy's literary legacy and as a writing retreat for future generations of writers. Certainly, during Al's lifetime, the A-frame was the de facto epicentre of English Canadian poetry, a refuge of sorts for a motley assortment of poets to swap literary ideas with an unlikely avuncular sage.

Through my own regrettable procrastination, I missed my chance to take part in that fine tradition, and perhaps that is why I feel so strongly about making sure we don't make the same mistake again: procrastination leads to lost opportunities. If we are to save the house, we must act now. To find out how you can support the Al Purdy A-frame Trust and help preserve a living piece of Canada's cultural heritage, please see the website and contact information at the back of this book.

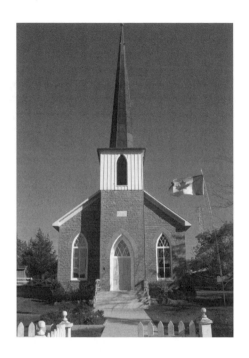

Wilderness Gothic

Al Purdy

Across Roblin Lake, two shores away,
they are sheathing the church spire
with new metal. Someone hangs in the sky
over there from a piece of rope,
hammering and fitting God's belly-scratcher,
working his way up along the spire
until there's nothing left to nail on—

AL PURDY

Perhaps the workman's faith reaches beyond:
touches intangibles, wrestles with Jacob,
replacing rotten timber with pine thews,
pounds hard in the blue cave of the sky,
contends heroically with difficult problems of
gravity, sky navigation and mythopocia,
his volunteer time and labour donated to God,
minus sick benefits of course on a non-union job—

Fields around are yellowing into harvest,
nestling and fingerling are sky and water borne,
death is yodelling quiet in green woodlots,
and bodies of three young birds have disappeared
in the sub-surface of the new county highway—

That picture is incomplete, part left out
that might alter the whole Dürer landscape:
gothic ancestors peer from medieval sky,
dour faces trapped in photograph albums escaping
to clop down iron roads with matched greys:
work-sodden wives groping inside their flesh
for what keeps moving and changing and flashing
beyond and past the long frozen Victorian day.
A sign of fire and brimstone? A two-headed calf
born in the barn last night? A sharp female agony?
An age and a faith moving into transition,
the dinner cold and new-baked bread a failure,
deep woods shiver and water drops hang pendant,
double-yolked eggs and the house creaks a little—

Something is about to happen. Leaves are still.
Two shores away, a man hammering in the sky.
Perhaps he will fall.

Support for the Al Purdy A-frame Trust

"I did visit the house and I did taste the wine. I can assure you that the preservation of this home is akin to the preservation of Canadian literary history. Should the plan to establish a poet-in-residence program be successful, the home will then also have a part in the future of Canadian literature."
– Margaret Atwood

"Al Purdy is one of Canada's most important twentieth century poets—the A-frame was not only a retreat for him and his family, but also for many of his colleagues in the writing community across the country. It holds both iconic and practical significance. Preserving it and making it available to Canadian writers as a place of retreat and creativity

(through an endowment for a poet-in-residence program) will help to ensure that not only Purdy's legacy will endure, but will also support and foster the wider legacy of poetry and literature, of art, in Canada."
– Sandra Barry, co-owner and the administrator of the Elizabeth Bishop House, NS

"It's a poor culture that bulldozes its history, or values its creators only for their income-generating abilities. Culture is more than money, more than the basic value of real estate. And that's why it's so important to save the Purdy house by the lake, the house where the many conversations of the past launched the literature of today. It's an important

touchstone that needs to be preserved. If we can't protect our past, how can we create our future?"
– Brian Brett

"It seems to me a most worthy project, Purdy's house being one of the more famous writer's houses in Canada and Purdy himself being such an important part of our literary history… In some ways, the house has already achieved a mythic status, becoming part of the literary geography of the country."
– Robert Currie, Poet Laureate of Saskatchewan

"He was a big man, both literally and metaphorically, and the office corridors seemed to course with energy when he came in, and I felt that people went about their business with extra pleasure because of his presence. I will always remember him with great affection… I hope we can prevent the destruction of the famous Purdy A-frame, and preserve it as an important piece of our history."
– Doug Gibson, editor of Douglas Gibson Books and former president and publisher of McClelland & Stewart

"I can't tell you how happy I was to hear that Al's A-frame might be preserved. I'll be glad to do anything I can to support this project—this is our heritage, after all."
– Kate Braid

"I was a friend of Al's & a guest at his & Euriethe's home a few times. They lived & ate simply, very much like my parents did, who were also Ontario-ites. So I felt at home. If there's a way to rescue that house from developers, Americans, those without any history, speculators, tight-arsed money-grubbers who verge on not being human at all because they value nothing but 'the bottom line' where 'the buck stops' & all that—then I'm in solidarity with such a plan."
– Phil Hall

"As someone who, as a young poet, benefited from Al and Eurithe Purdy's hospitality at the notorious A-frame in Ameliasburgh, I feel strongly that the A-frame project—to raise funds to purchase the property and create a poet-in-residence program—is a worthy one. (Here 'worthy' is a feebly inadequate word.) When Eurithe Purdy first spoke to me, a year ago, about her plans to sell the A-frame and her fears about what might become of the place, I told her, 'Someone ought to turn it into a writers' retreat. It would be *perfect*.' Eurithe, of course, had already thought of that—as had others. In fact a sort of synchronicity of intention seems to have gelled around the A-frame from the time Eurithe first spoke of selling it—a sign, I believe, that the project is a timely idea, and meant to be."
– Steven Heighton

"Canadians have, in the past, been incredibly proud of their country. But, somehow we have had a nasty habit of bulldozing our heritage. Despite protests, we bulldozed Hugh MacLennan's house. George Woodcock's home, which hosted decades of literary discussion, is gone. In all-nations report cards we score low on culture, history and heritage. We should go to work to save the A-frame and we've been given the opportunity. Let's show how important we regard fine people like Al Purdy."
– Mel Hurtig

"I think it is essential to preserve one of the most important literary landmarks in Canada, that of the home of the poet Al Purdy. What are we saying to the world as a country if we can erect a statue of him on the grounds of the Ontario Provincial Legislature, but destroy his house? Al Purdy's house on Roblin Lake is not only a part of our cultural heritage, but also an integral part of our history."
– Laurence Hutchman, Univeristé de Moncton

"As anyone knows who reads Al Purdy's poetry, that small spot in an odd corner of Eastern Ontario became the focus for his travels real and imaginary. He made the little lake the mirror of the universe. He built the house to write poetry in, and he filled it with poems."
– David Helwig

"Like the home of Emily Dickinson in the United States, the home of William Butler Yeats in Ireland, and Green Gables in PEI, Al Purdy's home deserves to be preserved for future generations as a tribute to Canada's literary legacy. Al Purdy is a major figure in the literature of the world and we must honour his contribution to the literary arts by preserving his home for posterity."
– John B. Lee, Poet Laureate of Brantford

"I want to add my name to the list of people who want to preserve Al Purdy's A-frame beside Roblin Lake, Ontario. It would be a crying shame if we let the weather and the current threatening climate for culture take down the home of one of our finest poets—someone who loved his Canada, and ought to be loved back for it."
– Marni Jackson, Chair, Literary
Journalism Program, Banff Centre;
Contributing Editor, *Walrus* Magazine

"This is a fragile piece of our literary heritage, and needs to be protected. As the first poet laureate for the City of Edmonton, I know that our poetic heritage is intensely local and yet national at the same time. If we don't have the local memories, there is nothing for us to remember as a country. Al is an important part of Canada's neurons, but we need to retain the physical spaces associated with him (and with other literary figures)."
– Alice Major

"This house served for many years as a Mecca for Canada's poets and writers who sought out the poet for his literary advice and counsel. Al brought Prince Edward County into the celebrated annals of our literary life. This house needs to be preserved and cherished, and definitely reincarnated for use by the literary community as a retreat or artistic centre."
– Seymour Mayne

"Canada needs Purdy's place in the Ontario woods, where his sweat and inspiration turned the dried-up intellectual blood of literature into a live vein in the Canadian mainstream; the country needs Purdy's place to continue that process into the future, needs his metamorphic cabin, where the sweat and inspiration of other poets can continue to change dry ideas into a fresh flow of blood through the veins of CanLit."
– George McWhirter, Vancouver's
inaugural Poet Laureate

"The Purdy house in Ontario was not only the locus of (and inspiration for) some of Al Purdy's own fine poetry, it also (during Al's lifetime) became a centre for the meeting of minds and a stimulus for even wider creative expression. It therefore holds a special place in Canadian cultural memory and it promises, if sustained, to provide a continuing venue for artistic expression. There is, therefore, intrinsic merit to preserving the house. More generally, the Purdy A-frame Project is emblematic of how the efforts of one generation of writers in Canada can help serve the needs of generations
to follow."
– W.H. (Bill) New, OC, FRSC

"The A-frame has itself become a poem. To allow it to be deconstructed and erased from the annals of our fledgling literary history cannot

be an option. We must help to again rewrite the A-frame's cultural potential as both a physical link to the last definitive era of Canadian poetry, and as a touchstone to yet-unwritten verse which will comprise its next."
– Owen Percy, University of Calgary

"The A-frame house besides having been Al's residence during the writing of many of his famous poems was also thematically central to the works. It was in addition a meeting place where Al's acolytes met and received unofficial mentorship and mutual connectivity. In that sense it has a cultural

importance that extends even beyond Purdy's works… What I like about the current effort to maintain the Purdy residence is that it is not intended to become some kind of a museum. Instead it will become an active present-day writer's residency. I love this double stroke of preserving our past while seeding our future."
– Robert Priest

"Perhaps the spirit of Al Purdy will enter the subconscious, or creative psyche of the writer in residence who resides in that rustic building… I have so many fond memories of that time I spent

there, drinking Al's home-made wine, and chatting with him in the wee hours of the morning. I hope that some patrons of Canlit come through with the money to purchase the building."
– Joe Rosenblatt

"The Purdy A-frame is more than a writer's home: it is living history, built and cared for by poetry. It must not go to waste. In honour of a man who was in so many ways larger than life, a man who encouraged and enthralled so many young writers (certainly my dear friend Bronwen Wallace was inspired to write by Al's groundbreaking language and form), the A-frame must be allowed to fulfill its purpose: to be a home for poets and a refuge for Canadian culture."
– Carolyn Smart, Director of Creative Writing, Queen's University

"The property is valuable in and of itself; as a writer's retreat and as a tribute to a great Canadian poet, this property is invaluable. I can think of no other property which has its associations with so much that has happened—and thus will happen—in the development of Canadian poetry. How extraordinarily fitting this would be if Al Purdy's A-frame could become the focal centre for writers, a place for retreat, and a place for the composition, as it has been in the past, for some of the finest poetry Canada has offered the world."
– David Staines

"We lose so many of our landmarks and so much of our physical history every year, it would be wonderful to preserve the house that Purdy built, lived and wrote in… Al and Eurithe's house should be saved! It should be made a national treasure."
– John Steffler, former Poet Laureate of Canada

Acknowledgements

Special thanks to Eurithe Purdy for her cooperation and contributions to this project. It could not have happened without her steadfast support.

Thanks to Jean Baird of the Al Purdy A-frame Trust for her enormous and often unsung efforts behind the scenes.

Thanks to Silas White and everyone at Harbour Publishing for being so actively and enthusiastically involved in every aspect of publishing this book.

Thanks to Dennis Lee, Stan Dragland, Howard White, George Galt, Joe Rosenblatt, Margaret Atwood, John Reeves, George Bowering, Duncan Patterson, David Helwig and Janet Lunn for their original contributions to this anthology.

Thanks to William Toye and the estate of F.R. Scott for permission to use a previously unpublished poem by Frank Scott.

Thanks to Linda Rogers, Russell Morton Brown, Wilfrid Laurier University Press, Geoff Heinricks, D.G. Jones, Steven Heighton, Seymour Mayne, David W. McFadden, Laurence Hutchman, and Harbour Publishing for their previously published contributions.

And thanks to Margaret Atwood, Sandra Barry, Kate Braid, Brian Brett, Robert Currie, Doug Gibson, Phil Hall, Steven Heighton, David Helwig, Mel Hurtig, Laurence Hutchman, John B. Lee, Marni Jackson, Alice Major, Seymour Mayne, George McWhirter, Bill New, Owen Percy, Robert Priest, Joe Rosenblatt, Carolyn Smart, David Staines, John Steffler, and others for their words of support.

Permissions

All poems by Al Purdy are used with permission.

The segments here titled "To Build a House!" "A Permanent Emergency," "And Acorn Came with Me to Roblin Lake," and "Maybe I Said Something that Annoyed Newlove," are excerpted from *Reaching for the Beaufort Sea* by Al Purdy (Harbour Publishing, 1993). Used with permission.

The segment titled "Ontario" by Al Purdy is excerpted from *Starting from Ameliasburgh: The Collected Prose of Al Purdy* (Harbour Publishing, 1995). Used with permission.

"This Inn Is Free" by F.R. Scott is used with the permission of William Toye, literary executor of the estate of F.R. Scott. Frank R. Scott Papers, Queen's University Archives. Coll. 5021.7, Box 4, Poetry Working Files, Reviews and Miscellaneous. [2 ts, one w/ revisions, one clean, later version; dated Apr. 1976]

"As the Dream Holds the Real: An Afterword" by Russell Morton Brown originally appeared in *The More Easily Kept Illusions: The Poetry of Al Purdy* (WLUP, 2006) and is used with the permission of the author and Wilfrid Laurier University Press.

The excerpt from Geoff Heinricks' *A Fool and Forty Acres* is used with the permission of the author, Anne McDermid & Associates, and McClelland & Stewart.

The excerpt from David W. McFadden's *A Trip Around Lake Ontario* is used with the permission of the author.

Photography / Image Credits

Title page (page 5) wood engraving by Alan Stein, originally included in the limited-edition book *Home Country* by Al Purdy, Church Street Press, 2000. Used with the permission of Alan Stein.

Pages 10, 16, 19, 22, 24, 25, 30, 32, 37, 40, 41, 42, 45, 57, 81, 87, 88, 89, 90, 93, 99, 105, 109, 110, 129, 136, 150 by Duncan Patterson.

Pages 12, 54, 72, 74, 78, 117, 147, 160 by Howard White.

Pages 13, 15, 26, 44, 46 (left), 47 (right), 55, 60, 108, 140 by Wendy Marshall.

Page 49 by Chris Miner.

Page 62 by John Reeves.

Page 97 courtesy Mary Hooper.

Page 128 by Jeremy Gilbert.

Page 144 by Kevin Kelly, www.kevinkellyphotography.com.

Page 152 by Bob Krieger.

All other photographs courtesy Eurithe Purdy.

Every reasonable effort has been made to seek permission from all known copyright holders for the use of their material. If any rights have been omitted, the publisher apologizes and will rectify this in any subsequent editions.

Please Support the Al Purdy A–frame Trust

To find out how you can support the Al Purdy A-frame Trust and help preserve a living piece of Canada's cultural heritage, please visit their website at www.alpurdy.ca or contact Jean Baird of the Al Purdy A-frame Trust at jeanbaird@shaw.ca or by calling 604-224-4898.

Cheques can be made out to The Al Purdy A-frame Trust and mailed to:

4403 West 11th Avenue
Vancouver, BC
V6R 2M2